OSPREY COMBAT AIRCRAFT

B-29 SUPERFORTRESS UNITS OF THE KOREAN WAR

SERIES EDITOR: TONY HOLMES

OSPREY COMBAT AIRCRAFT • 42

B-29 SUPERFORTRESS UNITS OF THE KOREAN WAR

Robert F Dorr

OSPREY
PUBLISHING

Front cover
When the piercing yellow-white beams of North Korean radar-guided searchlights converged on the silver-black hull of a B-29 bomber on a night mission, the result was always trouble for the 11-man crew of the aircraft. On this nocturnal sortie above the 38th Parallel, depicted in artwork specially for this volume by Mark Postlethwaite, the aircraft under scrutiny from the ground is Wichita-built B-29-95-BW Superfortress 45-21822 (c/n 13716), bearing the name *HEAVENLY LADEN*. The bomber was assigned to Capt Raymond M Lajeunesse's crew, who were in turn part of the 98th Bombardment Group's 344th Bombardment Squadron (Medium), flying out of Yokota Air Base in Japan.

Entering frontline service near the end of World War 2, this veteran B-29 flew a considerable number of sorties before coming to an untimely end on 29 January 1952. Suffering an engine fire whilst returning from yet another mission over North Korea, the bomber crashed five miles west of Yokohama, on the outskirts of Tokyo. The crew all baled out successfully

Back cover profile
B-29-35-MO 44-27288 *ATOMIC TOM* of the 30th BS/19th BG, based at Kadena Air Base, Okinawa, in 1950. *ATOMIC TOM* was one of four Superfortresses that bombed the Seoul railway station and Han River bridges on the afternoon of 28 June 1950 – fully six hours before US President Harry S Truman gave approval for offensive operations to begin in Korea. A veteran of numerous combat missions during the Korean War, this aircraft was attacked by MiG-15s on 12 April 1951. Despite the communist fighters inflicting significant battle damage, *ATOMIC TOM* was eventually repaired and returned to operations. It did not survive the war, however

DEDICATION
This book is dedicated to Airman 2nd Class Donald Wilson (1933-1952), who gave his life for others who fly and fight

First published in Great Britain in 2003 by Osprey Publishing
Elms Court, Chapel Way, Botley, Oxford, OX2 9LP

© 2003 Osprey Publishing Limited

ISBN 1 84176 654 2

Edited by Tony Holmes
Page design by Tony Truscott
Cover Artwork by Mark Postlethwaite
Aircraft Profiles and Scale Drawings by Mark Styling
Index by Alan Rutter
Origination by Grasmere Digital Imaging, Leeds, UK
Printed by Stamford Press PTE, Singapore

03 04 05 06 07   10 9 8 7 6 5 4 3 2 1

ACKNOWLEDGEMENTS
The author would like to thank the following B-29 veterans who assisted with this book:

Ancil Baker (Fifteenth Air Force), Russ Beard (307th BG), Frank 'Bud' Farrell (93rd BS/19th BG), Dick Ferrell (307th BG), Richard E 'Gene' Fisher, (30th BS/ 19th BG), Herb Harper (98th BG), Vernon R 'Bob' Hudder (344th BS/98th BG), Richard Iler (345th BS/98th BG), John Kalogeris, Edward 'Ebbie' LeMaster (93rd BS/19th BG), E J 'Mac' McGill (28th BS/19th BG), Jesse Richey (345th BS/98th BG), Ralph Livengood (30th BS/19th BG), Charles 'Chuck' Rees (93rd BS/19th BG) and Roland T Speckman (344th BS/98th BG)

The author would also like to thank Arthur Block, Bob Crevisour, John T Jones, Ted Kalogeris, Ray Lent, Thomas Schipper and Norman Taylor.

Finally, the author wishes to thank the Air Force History Support Office for giving him permission to quote from the US government history *The United States Air Force in Korea 1950-1953* by Robert F Futrell, Vernon R 'Bob' Hudder for permission to quote from his war memoir *The Brush of AngelWings* and Frank 'Bud' Farrell for permission to quote from his war memoir *No Sweat*, which is available from www.1stbooks.com.

Profile artist Mark Styling wishes to acknowledge the help given to him by Bill Banks, Darrel W Cooper, Kim Comeau (Assistant Crew Chief on *RAZ'N HELL*), 'Sparky' Corradina, Clyde Durham, Frank 'Bud' Farrell, Bob Mann, Wayland Mayo, Dan McElhiney, James S Peters Sr, Don Rubendall, Brian Schneider (19th BG webmaster), Warren Thompson, Dewey Thomas, Ford Tolbert and Sallyann Wagoner, and her website *B-29 Superfortress – Then and Now*, and the contributors to its Discussion List.

For a catalogue of all Osprey Publishing titles please contact us at:

Osprey Direct UK, PO Box 140, Wellingborough, Northants, NN8 2FA, UK
E-mail: **info@ospreydirect.co.uk**

Osprey Direct USA, c/o MBI Publishing, 729 Prospect Ave, PO Box 1, Osceola, WI 54020, USA
E-mail: **info@ospreydirectusa.com**

CONTENTS

1950

In the early hours of Sunday, 25 June 1950, in darkness and driving rain, North Korean armed forces crossed the 38th Parallel at half-a-dozen locations. Some 90,000 troops and hundreds of Russian-made T-34 medium tanks spearheaded the invasion of South Korea. The North Koreans also threw their air force, commanded by Maj Gen Wang Yon, into the battle.

Author F Scott Fitzgerald said, 'There are no second acts in American lives'. This quote, however, did not apply to US combat aircraft, for the Korean War would quickly become 'Act II' for many familiar aircraft types – among them the four-engined Boeing B-29 Superfortress.

Five years after the B-29 had razed Japan's home islands and introduced the world to the atomic age, a small number of the bombers remained on duty in the Far East. At Andersen Air Force Base, Guam, in the Marianas Islands, the legendary 19th Bombardment Group (Medium) was operating the bomber, its 'label' only recently having changed from 'very heavy' to 'medium'. The men of the 19th BG took perverse pride in not being members of the relatively new Strategic Air Command (SAC), their bombers lacking the circles, squares and letters that marked the tails of SAC aircraft. The crews' approach to life was wholly different too. While SAC valued discipline, the men of the 19th BG were unkempt and irreverent, and would remain so.

The 31st Photo Reconnaissance Squadron (Very Long Range), equipped with the photo-reconnaissance RB-29, formerly known as the F-13A, called Naha, Okinawa, home. This unit would soon be joined by the 91st Strategic Reconnaissance Squadron (SRS), which would eventually absorb it. Here, a more traditional set of markings was visible, with the reconnaissance squadrons wearing a letter X enclosed in a circle.

Various bases in the region also boasted detachments of the 2nd and 3rd Air Rescue Squadrons, equipped with the SB-17G Flying Fortress and SB-29 Superfortress search and rescue aircraft, both capable of carrying lifeboats. Other units boasted WB-29 Superfortress weather reconnaissance aircraft.

In the half-decade between World War 2 and Korea, the US Air Force went from being part of the Army to being an independent service branch, the threat of atomic war began to loom, and jet-powered aeroplanes began to replace those with propellers. But the B-29 Superfortress remained the bulwark of the US strategic force. This previously unpublished glimpse at a 1949 line-up of B-29s at Smokey Hill Air Force Base, Kansas, typifies the era (*Frank C Fox*)

RB-29A-45-BN Superfortress 44-61727 served with the 91st SRS, stationed at Johnson Air Base, Japan. It is seen in flight over the Sea of Japan in 1950, just weeks prior to the outbreak of the Korean War (*Mike Moffitt*)

SB-29 Superfortress 44-84084 sits on the ramp between missions. This search and rescue version of the bomber is seen without the lifeboat it was capable of carrying beneath the fuselage. The SB-29 flew vital rescue missions throughout the fighting from 1950 to 1953. (*US Air Force*)

Official figures show that the equivalent of nine combat wings (out of 48 worldwide) was stationed in the Far East, with Superfortress strength on 25 June 1950 consisting of 22 B-29s, 24 WB-29s, six RB-29s and four SB-29s. These were part of a force of 533 aircraft which also included 365 F-80 Shooting Stars, 25 RF-80 Shooting Stars, 32 F-82 Twin Mustangs, 25 B-26 Invaders, 26 C-54 Skymasters and 23 SB-17s.

It would be almost impossible to exaggerate how unprepared the US Air Force was for the Korean War. As pointed out by author Clay Blair in *The Forgotten War: America in Korea 1950-1953*, during World War 2, the Army Air Forces possessed 218 combat groups, 68,400 aircraft and 2.3 million men. In that war, the AAF lost about 55,000 men in combat, or about 20,000 more than the entire US Marine Corps. At the end of the war, Gen Henry H 'Hap' Arnold recommended a post-war force of 70 combat groups and 400,000 men. Arnold also advocated a rapid transition to jet aircraft.

According to Blair, President Harry S Truman distrusted airmen. He wrote that Truman 'demeaned them as "glamour boys" who made wild claims. He believed their aeroplanes were exorbitantly – and needlessly – expensive. Despite the recommendations of several blue-ribbon committees and others, which seconded Arnold's concept of a 70-group Air Force, Truman categorically rejected it as excessively expensive and continued to oppose it with all his main and might'. Truman apparently wanted the Air Force, which became an independent service branch between wars, to have no more than 48 combat groups totalling 6869 aeroplanes, and in fact its strength was considerably smaller when North Korea attacked. In fairness to Truman, it must be added that his decision to defend South Korea was made without hesitation, and is viewed today as one of the most courageous calls of his presidency.

The North Korean invasion threw B-29 Superfortress crews into action almost immediately. But it also instigated some of those fights that occur

7

General of the Army Douglas MacArthur was both the US and UN Commander in Korea (*US Army*)

Lt Gen George E 'Strat' Stratemeyer was commander of Far East Air Forces, reporting to Gen Douglas MacArthur, when the Korean War began on 25 June 1950. Stratemeyer was an experienced bomber commander and B-29 pilot, with an affable manner that hid a tough, determined personality (*Art Lent*)

whenever American forces go to war – 'turf' battles. Before crews could fly into enemy flak and deliver their bombs to the target, the brass had to sort out who was giving orders and how the chain of command worked.

In June 1950, Gen Douglas MacArthur was the American theatre commander in the Far East, and as such he headed up US Far East Command (FEC). MacArthur's title was Commander-in-Chief, Far East Command (CINCFEC). His responsibility was the defence of Japan, the Philippines and the East Asian region, but this duty did not include Korea. US forces had withdrawn from Korea two years earlier, and American policy makers seem to have ruled out the possibility of trouble there.

When the fighting began, and President Truman made the decision to shed US blood in defence of South Korea, the Pentagon expanded MacArthur's responsibilities and those of his subordinates.

AIR COMMAND

The B-29 bombers already in the combat theatre belonged to Far East Air Forces (FEAF), predecessor of the command that is known in today's jargon as Pacific Air Forces (PACAF). Under MacArthur, the air commander at FEAF, which airmen pronounced to rhyme with 'leaf,' was Lt Gen George E Stratemeyer. Described by historian Robert F Futrell as 'genial', with 'something of the air of a jolly college professor', Stratemeyer had a mild-mannered appearance that could be deceiving. He was a tough bomber general who had been air commander in the China Burma India theatre during World War 2.

One component under 'Strat' was the Twentieth Air Force at Kadena Air Base, Okinawa. Throughout the Korean War, the island of Okinawa was administered by the US, and did not revert to Japanese control for a further 20 years. Maj Gen A C Kincaid finished his tour of duty as Twentieth commander in the first days of the war, and was relieved on 31 July 1950 by Maj Gen Ralph Stearley. Although the Twentieth had been responsible for all B-29s in the final days of the war against Japan, by 1950 this numbered air force was a mere shadow of its former self.

Moreover, the Twentieth no longer owned the entire American B-29 force. The RB-29s already in the combat zone and most Superfortress units that arrived after the war began were the property of SAC, led throughout the Korean era by Gen Curtis E LeMay. LeMay, of course, had been the Twentieth's commander during the 'big war'. He was fiercely protective of his SAC crews, and had no intention of placing them under MacArthur, Stratemeyer, Stearley or anyone else.

It was largely due to LeMay's efforts that the United States remained ready for a global nuclear war with the Soviet Union, but it was also LeMay's intransigence that prevented bomber crews in the Korean War from operating any bomber newer than the B-29, even though the B-36, B-47 and B-50 were all in service when the conflict started, or soon afterwards. The first production-standard B-47A Stratojet bomber, in fact, completed its first flight on the very day the Korean War began, but it will not reappear in this narrative for it never reached the combat zone.

To this day, a myth persists among B-29 veterans that there was an unwritten agreement between Washington and Moscow about using only outdated equipment in Korea. Said former S/Sgt Richard 'Dick' Iler, a left blister gunner with the 345th BS/98th BG;

'We thought there was a tacit understanding that both sides would use obsolete equipment. There was a tacit understanding that we wouldn't use our best stuff and they wouldn't either.'

This myth is based in part on yet another myth – that there were modern Soviet nightfighters, available in force, that were purposely kept out of the Korean fighting. In fact, there never was such an understanding, tacit or otherwise, and there were no such nightfighters. Except in the first months of the war, the latest Soviet aeroplanes were always available on the other side, even if B-36s, B-47s and B-50s were withheld from American bomber crews.

To understand what the B-29 achieved in Korea, it is useful to remember what the B-36 did not do.

On the day the Korean War began, six examples of the mighty B-36 (called the Peacemaker in literature today, but never identified by that name during its time in service) were in Hawaii on a 'show of force' tour. The big bombers belonged to the 7th BG at Carswell Air Force Base, in Texas, but were basking in the sunshine at Hickam Air Force Base, Hawaii, when the fighting began. Ironically, the group's past included a period when Stratemeyer had been its commander from 1936 to 1938.

Radio operator Sgt Arthur Block of the group's 492nd BS was one of many B-36 crewmen who read a headline in the Saturday, 24 June 1950 *Honolulu Star Bulletin* describing how they would soon rehearse their mission. 'B-36s IN HAWAII TO 'BOMB' US CITIES ON TRIP HOME', proclaimed the headline. Across the international dateline, where it was a day later, men were already dying in the Korean mud.

'Once we knew the United States was involved in the fighting we were certain we would be ordered to attack North Korea', said Block in an interview. It never occurred to him that the US government had not known that the war was coming. He assumed he was in Hawaii because of the fighting in Korea, and not merely by coincidence.

At this juncture, Block's B-36 unit had never studied, trained or practiced in the delivery of conventional bombs, but the B-36 could

Gen Curtis LeMay (centre left, wearing the buttoned up tunic) steps off a C-54 Skymaster for a visit to B-29 squadrons at Yokota Air Base, Japan. As commander-in-chief of Strategic Air Command, LeMay was the US Air Force's top bomber general, and was considered 'the boss', even by those in B-29 squadrons that reported to Far East Air Forces. His command supplied two B-29 Superfortress bomb groups and an F-84 Thunderjet fighter group to Korean action – and, on a temporary basis, a handful of RB-50G Superfortress reconnaissance aircraft. LeMay tried to keep the Air Force focused on the global threat from the Soviet Union while Korean fighting persisted (US Air Force)

have quickly shed its nuclear mission and carried high explosive ordnance if a different command arrangement had prevailed. At the Non-commissioned Officers Club in Honolulu, Block and his buddies talked about how they would soon be bombing North Korea. It never happened. LeMay ordered the B-36s home.

The control of some bombers by SAC during the Korean War (like the control of all bombers by SAC during the Vietnam conflict years later) had an impact on every decision about priorities, and assured a

No air base in the Far East offered maintainers the luxury of performing routine work on the Superfortress indoors. Here, Cpl Charlie Williams (far left) is working on the number one engine of a B-29 of the 345th BS/98th BG at Yokota (*Jess Richey*)

persistent rivalry between the two commands responsible for identical B-29 missions in Korea. LeMay's concern about husbanding his resources was legendary and commendable (even today, the USAF benefits from the frugal way he employed his tanker force in its early years), but it happened for the simple reason that a potential war with the Soviet Union enjoyed higher priority than a very real war in Korea. Sometimes the relationship was cooperative and supportive, but sometimes FEAF and SAC seemed to be on different wavelengths.

Throughout the Korean conflict, the B-29 force never came under a single command. This had an impact on the condition and appearance of the B-29s in the combat zone. 'The difference between FEAF and SAC aircraft and airmen was like night and day', said former 1Lt Michael Curphey, an FEAF pilot. 'We had the oldest, grungiest stuff in the Air Force, and were kind of proud of our rowdy, unseemly appearance. In contrast, the SAC boys had creases in their flightsuits, spit-shined brogans and aeroplanes that were as silvery as a new toy'.

Former 1Lt Ralph Livengood of Charlotte, North Carolina, who had been a navigator aboard B-17s in World War 2 and then saw further action with B-29s in Korea, was one of the FEAF crowd;

'We may have lacked spit and polish, but we knew our stuff. The 19th had flown the B-29 in World War 2 and was still stationed on Guam when the Korean War began. They transferred immediately to Kadena Air Base. They were the first group to fly B-29s in Korea, and were using the same aeroplanes that had been flown in World War 2, with the same colours, the same nose art, the whole works. We were told that one aeroplane in the group had 200 missions to its credit on the day the Korean War started. Later, SAC groups arrived with virtually new B-29s that had been carefully preserved in mothballs since the end of World War 2.'

EARLY MISSIONS

Retired M/Sgt Richard E 'Gene' Fisher of Hickory, North Carolina, who was a private first class (Pfc) and B-29 gunner at the time, remembers being 'pretty much surprised' by everything that was happening in the 30th BS/19th BG (Livengood's squadron);

'One Sunday morning (25 June 1950) we were relaxing behind our barracks in Guam when they came and told us to load up the guns, ammunition and bombs. They moved us to Kadena Air Base – ten to twelve aeroplanes per squadron, and more than 30 altogether. As gunners, we did not attend the main briefings, so even though the North Koreans were already south of Seoul, we were not completely clear on what was happening. We flew a mission where we went down low and bombed some tanks, and then we gunners were ordered to strafe the area. It didn't dawn on me until that moment that we were in a shooting war. I can still remember the sense of combat, the confusion on the interphone, the smell of gunpowder, the vibrations and the noise.'

The 19th BG flew its first combat mission on 28 June 1950, some six hours before President Truman authorised intervention in Korea. There were four Superfortresses on the mission – *Double Whammy* (44-87734), *THE OUTLAW* (42-65306), *Lucky Dog* (44-86370) and *Atomic Tom* (44-69682). Not one of these aircraft would survive the Korean War. They attacked the Seoul railway station (a seemingly indestructible, red-brick building that was badly damaged but never lost its exterior facade throughout the war) and the bridges that crossed the Han River on the southern edge of the capital. A published source which states that the first strike took place 24 hours earlier is apparently in error, for the 19th BG was still packing and moving from Guam to Okinawa the previous day.

It is unclear how much happened on that first mission. At the time, it was reported that the four B-29s loitered over roads near Seoul. In the words of historian Robert F Futrell, who later wrote the definitive history of the US Air Force in Korea for the US government, the bombardiers 'toggled out bombs against anything that looked to be worth a bomb'. MacArthur was trying to make a show of force. It is possible that he did not yet understand the size or speed of the North Korean assault.

The next day (29th) a communications glitch prevented B-29s from again bombing the Han River bridges, across which the enemy would pour troops after seizing Seoul, but the bombers did attack Kimpo airfield and the Seoul railway station to make them less useful to the foe.

B-29 CREW COMPOSITION

For the next three years B-29 Superfortress crews would fight a difficult war in an ageing aircraft. The composition of a B-29 crew varied slightly according to the mission, but it typically included 11 men. Moving from nose to tail, those forward of the bomb-bay, and the tunnel above it, were:
– the bombardier, who sat farthest forward in the B-29, and also acted as nose gunner.
– the pilot, or aircraft commander (AC), who occupied the front left seat on the flight deck.
– the co-pilot, who flew the aircraft from the right seat
– the flight engineer, who sat behind the pilot facing an instrument panel used to monitor engine performance, and who also served as the top turret gunner.
– the navigator, who sat to the left of the forward turret behind the two pilots. He had a window (which didn't amount to much – 'a day or night indicator' one navigator called it!) and an astrodome to use when performing celestial navigation.

1Lt Roy F Dobbins demonstrates the bombardier's position in the forward nose of a B-29 Superfortress (*US Air Force*)

Tail gunner Sgt Kenneth W Roberts of the 344th BS/98th BG looks out from his Superfortress at Yokota. This photograph was one of a series of pictures requested by his wing commander, Col Charles B Westover. During World War 2, most B-29s were delivered with a 20 mm cannon and two 0.50-cal machine guns in the tail. The cannon never worked well, and by the time of the Korean War the tail gun position was equipped with machine guns only (*Roland T Speckman*)

– the radio operator, who sat behind the top turret with no window in a very narrow, confined space.

The crew members located aft of the bomb-bay, and the tunnel above it, were:

– the left gunner, who was also the left scanner. He fired guns from a remote control in the left astrodome.

– the right gunner.

– the central fire control (CFC) gunner, who rode in a 'barber's chair', looked out from atop the fuselage, and coordinated the firing of the remotely-controlled guns by various gunners.

– the radar operator, who sat in an enclosed compartment in the back and had no windows.

– the tail gunner, who rode facing to the rear, and manned the tail guns.

HURTING THE ENEMY

Early strikes by B-29 Superfortresses had some impact on the advancing North Koreans, bomber crews willingly running the gauntlet of enemy gunfire while being tossed about in a cramped interior with the comfort level of a Spam can. As previously mentioned, many of the B-29s in-theatre were 'high hour' aircraft, making them difficult to maintain and keep aloft. Further, poor intelligence and targeting information, and poor communications, made it impossible to change targets at short notice.

Nevertheless, Stratemeyer and his staff concluded that the B-29 was effective when the 19th BG once again attacked the bridges spanning the Han River on 1 July. Well aware that bridges are among the most difficult targets to demolish with aerial bombardment, Stratemeyer ordered B-29 crews to bomb individually, and continue to drop single bombs if they saw hits. The river ran along Seoul's southern outskirts (since then, the city has expanded to surround it), and the Superfortresses apparently inflicted severe damage on two of the four spans. In retrospect, it seems wasteful to use a B-29 against a bridge, but Stratemeyer was satisfied, and he believed that the effort helped to slow the enemy advance.

On 2 July, acting on a report that a concentration of 65 aircraft was based at Yonpo airfield, near Hungnam on the east coast of North Korea, FEAF sent ten B-29s of the 29th BG to attack. But the bomber crews sighted only 16 aircraft on the ground, and the ordnance they dropped apparently damaged none of them. Elsewhere, other action by US Air Force and Navy aeroplanes was whittling away at the North Korean air force, which would not last long as a serious threat in the skies.

On 3 July, SAC's Fifteenth Air Force was ordered to send the B-29s of the 22nd and 92nd BGs to the Far East on temporary duty. Within a few months, they were to be replaced by the 98th and 307th BGs, which would remain in the combat zone for the remainder of the war.

BOMBER COMMAND

In an attempt to patch up differences between FEAF and SAC, the USAF established Far East Air Forces Bomber Command (Provisional) on 8 July under the command of Maj Gen Emmett 'Rosie' O'Donnell, who was yet another veteran of the B-29 campaign in World War 2 (see *Osprey Combat Aircraft 33 – B-29 Superfortress Units of World War 2* for further details). O'Donnell's new command immediately took charge of all B-29 operations during the Korean War. The machines and people still belonged to the separate commands, however, and throughout the war there would be cultural, leadership and personal differences between FEAF and SAC bomber crews.

Ironically, as one B-29 crewmember recalls, the Superfortress crews initially had to do more than just fly the bombers into combat;

'There had been a RIF (reduction in force) a few months earlier. Flying crews had to load, fuel and fly the aircraft. That's how short we were. In early July 1950, we bombed the runway and buildings at Pyongyang, doing some damage. When the war settled into place, we flew two missions a day over North Korea starting at 0500 hrs. What with a briefing, flying, debriefing and briefing for a subsequent night flight, it was a long, long day, and there was not much time for sleep.'

Almost immediately, in the D Ring of the Pentagon where the Air Staff resided, ideas were discussed which, because of the Cold War, were never to materialise. An officer pointed out that there would soon be a number of B-50s available, these machines being an improved, longer-ranged version of the B-29 that were coming fresh out of the Boeing factory. They were a little faster, a little easier to maintain and, above all, they were new.

It was decided early, and very firmly, that the new B-50s were to go to stateside SAC units, which had the all-important mission of remaining ready for an atomic war with the Russians. The B-50, like the B-47s which became operational soon afterwards, was destined never to be used in Korea – except in its RB-50G reconnaissance version. Americans might bleed and die on a gnarled Asian peninsula, but the confrontation with the USSR had first call on new US technology and equipment.

M/Sgt Carl W Toole works on the tail gun installation of a B-29, having first removed the upper portion of the tail cone housing. As previously mentioned, the Superfortress came out of the factory fitted with two 0.50-cal machine guns and one 20 mm cannon in the tail position, although by 1950 the rear turret usually boasted just three 'fifties'. Toole was a veteran of 88 combat missions in World War 2, and he would complete a further 52 in Korea. In the latter conflict, he served with both the 29th and 98th BGs (*US Air Force*)

KOREA FIGHTING

For many B-29 crews sent into war from bases in Japan, operating with the FEAF was nothing new. 'We had been here once before, so we had a headquarters all set up', remembers one of the men who arrived at Yokota Air Base on 12 July 1950 in a Superfortress. 'We were the first SAC organisation that was alerted. We were very experienced crews already, and we had done a TDY (temporary duty) in Japan once before. A lot of us had previously flown the B-29 against Japan. Initially, our concern was that there was a dearth of targets'.

When the 19th BG was ordered to provide close support to beleaguered American ground troops on 10 July, it did more harm than good. Ten B-29s despatched to attack mechanised targets of opportunity were unable to contact FEAF's frontline tactical air support parties. It also developed that B-29s had been sent to attack vehicles, tanks and troop concentrations that would have been more vulnerable to B-26 Invaders, while the smaller B-26s had been assigned to strike bridges – ideally suited as B-29 targets.

On 11 July, eight B-29s assigned to a tactical mission were at last able to make contact with ground parties and strike North Korean forces in Wonju, Pyongytaek and Chunchon, achieving good results.

It appears that the first Superfortress lost in combat belonged to the 28th BS/19th BG, the aircraft going down on 12 July. Navigator 1Lt Donald Brous, interviewed by Warren Thompson for the April 2003 issue of *Wings* magazine, strongly suggested that the Superfortress's No 3

'HELL ON WINGS' reads the sign outside the headquarters building of the 345th BS/98th BG at Yokota (*Richard Iler*)

engine was shot out by a North Korean Yakovlev Yak-9 fighter that briefly appeared behind the bomber. The pilot feathered the engine, but could not extinguish the blaze. After the bombardier made an apparent 'lone-wolf' decision to bale out over enemy territory, thus becoming the first B-29 prisoner of war, Brous told Thompson;

'We reached an altitude of about 3000 ft, at which time we were given the bale-out signal. We were over the Yellow Sea, west of Seoul, offshore from the town of Songmo-ri. The aircraft commander, co-pilot, flight engineer and I baled out through the nose wheel well, while the rest of the crew went out through the bomb-bay. One of our guys back in the aft section was never heard from after the incident. I wound up in the water and managed to deploy my one-man dinghy. Shortly thereafter, a boat came out from shore and picked me up. Most of the crew was safely in Japan within 24 hours.'

The USAF's official account of this loss lists the downed aircraft as B-29A 44-69866. In fact, aircraft 44-69866 was a Wichita-built B-29, not a B-29A.

On 14 July Superfortresses took off from Yokota at nine-minute intervals to attack advancing North Korean troops that appeared on the verge of overwhelming the 24th Infantry Division near Taejon. This maximum effort continued the next day, and crews reported that they had achieved 'fair to good results'. Three B-29s bombed Kimpo airfield, near Seoul, on the 15th, the base now being in enemy hands. It was hoped that this raid would make the airfield less useful to the North Korea Ilyushins and Yaks. As it turned out, this effort may have been unnecessary, for the enemy apparently never had any intention of moving aircraft that far south.

YAK ATTACK

Pfc Gene Fisher, a gunner with the 30th BS/19th BG who was uprooted from Guam to Kadena at the start of the Korean War, flew one of his most memorable missions on 19 July. 'We were just a few weeks into this war and didn't know a lot about what was happening' he related to the author. He had come to the Far East at the beginning of the year, before the outbreak of fighting, and 'had never heard of Korea, and didn't have any idea I would ever be flying over Korea'.

That day, Fisher was left gunner in the crew of Capt (later, Maj) John W Edenbo, one of the oldest pilots in the squadron, and a combat veteran from World War 2. Their aircraft was *Bug's Ball Buster*, alias Renton-built B-29-40-BN Superfortress 44-61638.

'We were not assigned a target that day, but were told to go and bomb targets of opportunity. We were approaching the bridges along the Han River, near Seoul, with 35 500-lb bombs in our bays, when three Yak pilots came right up at us while we were on the bombing run. They were very quick-moving little prop-driven fighters, and they also seemed to be very well briefed. It was clear that they had some respect for our guns.

'They came in from behind, but dropped back out of range of our guns. We were shooting at them anyway. We took hits in the bomb-bay, and every one of us was thinking about that load of bombs, and what they could do to our aeroplane if they exploded. Capt Edenbo dropped the bombs (it is not clear from Fisher's recollection whether they were dropped on a bridge or merely jettisoned) and dived into a cloud. By then

we had been hit in several places by gunfire from the Yaks, and there was a lot of chatter on the interphone.'

Long after the Yak-9s had departed, the crew of *Bug's Ball Buster* was in crisis. 'From up front somebody said on the intercom that they needed the first aid kit. It was next to me, so I grabbed it and went through the tunnel over the bomb-bay to the front of the B-29.

'On the flight deck there were bullet holes everywhere. We had lost pressurisation. Capt Edenbo had gotten hit. The bullets punctured the forward fuselage where *Bugs Bunny* was painted on the right side

There is a large round bowling ball between the words *Bug's* and *Buster* (just behind our favourite 'wabbit'), which is why this aircraft was named *Bug's Ball Buster*. Officially B-29A-40-BN Superfortress 44-61638 of the 30th BS/19th BG, this aircraft survived a 1950 battle with a Yak-9 fighter and remained in the frontline well into 1952, as the 19th BG continued its efforts against North Korea (*Gene Fisher*)

of the aircraft. One bullet had shattered glass and thrown it into Edenbo's face. I'll never forget the sight of him lying out there on the floor. There was blood all over his face. I thought he was dead. I took the first aid kit and we tried to help him. Fortunately, there was an extra pilot aboard so we still had two pilots to try to get back to Kadena. Looking back later, I don't know why we didn't divert to South Korea or western Japan instead.

'Going back, we couldn't get the rear bomb-bay doors closed, which meant that all the flight characteristics of the B-29 were out of whack. The electrical systems were shot away. We had no radio. We got into a storm but, somehow, that aeroplane kept going all the way back to Kadena. We didn't fully appreciate how much damage we had until we got landed – there were well over 100 holes in the bomber. Edenbo survived, but that mission was a tough one.'

Gene Fisher held the opinion that the B-29 was underpowered, and believed the poor characteristics of the aircraft on take-off affected morale. 'We lost a lot of aeroplanes on take-off. Not everybody thought that was justified. All this time, we knew there were newer bombers, yet we were still flying B-29s.'

A typical Superfortress was powered by four 2200 hp Wright R-3350-23-23A/-41 Cyclone 18 turbocharged radial piston engines driving four-bladed propellers, which was enough to assure a maximum speed of 358 mph at 25,000 ft, and a service ceiling of 31,850 ft. Despite these impressive figures, they were nowhere near high enough to make Fisher, and many of his crewmates, believe that a fully loaded B-29 had sufficient power when beginning its long and often ponderous take-off roll.

As part of the continuing campaign against the enemy's air arm, on 20 July Stratemeyer diverted 14 B-29s from ground support and sent them to crater the runways at two airfields near the North Korean capital, Pyongyang. That day, B-29 gunners fired bursts that drove off two North Korean fighters after they inflicted only minor damage on a Superfortress in a brief aerial engagement.

Nevertheless, the bomber crews were spooked by the threat of Yak fighters, and 22nd BG commander Col James V Edmundson told gunners to fire at any unidentified aircraft that came within range and pointed its nose at one of the bombers. When four fighters appeared near one of Edmundson's B-29s, both the tail gunner and the central fire-control gunner opened fire on them. One aircraft was hit and the pilot baled out. Everyone in the bomber crew identified their 'attacker' as a Yak-9, but it was, in reality, a Supermarine Seafire Mk 47 from the British aircraft carrier HMS *Triumph*.

This was not the only time Edmundson had things wrong. Speaking of the early bombing campaign, he said, 'Our bombing should have been good. We didn't have any opposition and the bombardiers had all the time in the world to make their bomb runs'. This was briefly true in the summer of 1950, but the situation would not last.

BRANCHING OUT

Most early B-29 attacks were against tactical targets such as tank concentrations, troops, truck traffic, arsenals and supply dumps. There was little flak or air opposition, but the raids were not very effective since the B-29 was not well suited to the tactical role. Command, control and communications problems hindered any sort of coordinated approach to the air campaign, and this would remain the case throughout most of the Korean War. Indeed, US Navy aircraft did not have radios that were compatible with those of the US Air Force and Army, and on several occasions B-29 strikes were cancelled or diverted because proper communications could not be made to work.

In Tokyo, MacArthur's Far East Command Target Selection Committee haggled furiously about where to send the overburdened B-29 crews and what to do with them. With three American divisions struggling to defend a decreasing patch of South Korea from nine North Korean divisions, MacArthur's Army generals argued that all B-29 strikes should be flown over the frontlines, where the four-engined bombers could directly support beleaguered friendly troops. Air Force generals wanted to go deep, crossing the 38th Parallel into North Korea and disrupting the enemy's industry and supply lines by attacking strategic targets.

In Washington, USAF chief of staff Gen Hoyt S Vandenberg was studying FEAF's needs for aircraft, men and equipment. Although the Korean War never received the same priority in Washington that was given to the expected atomic war with the Soviet Union, Vandenberg himself was eager to support Stratemeyer and other commanders in the field. 'We want', he said, 'to insure the position of the USAF in this job that is being done over there (and) be sure that it is being done with the very best equipment in the shortest time. When a request comes in, that request must be fully met'. Vandenberg felt the entire USAF in 1950 was 'a shoestring air force', and thus wanted more resources at every level for both Korea and the Cold War.

Against some opposition, on 3 July 1950 Vandenberg secured approval from the Joint Chiefs of Staff (JCS) to move the 22nd and 92nd BGs to the Far East. The other members of the JCS warned Vandenberg that they wanted to see B-29s attacking strategic targets, not providing close air support for troops.

On 29 July, the JCS proposed to send two additional B-29 groups for 30 days of temporary duty in the Far East on the condition – which is still controversial today – that they be used against strategic targets. SAC alerted the Fifteenth Air Force's 98th and 307th BGs to prepare for war. MacArthur (who was often criticised for having not used his bombers more effectively in the Philippines when the Japanese attacked on 8 December 1941) found the formal decision to send the SAC B-29s a 'highly desirable' move.

RAILWAY WORK

Following through on a wish expressed by MacArthur, on 16 July 1950, FEAF CO Maj Gen 'Rosie' O'Donnell launched 47 B-29s of the 19th and 22nd BGs against the Seoul railway marshalling yards, while eight Superfortresses of the 82nd BG went after more tactical targets.

The mission to enemy-occupied Seoul destroyed rolling stock, cut the main rail lines and set fire to the large repair and assembly shops. The B-29s assigned to tactical targets proved less useful. Three of the bomber crews mistook their location and attacked a town on the southern side of the bomb line, killing 22 civilians. The results of this mission, and overall results against tactical targets generally, persuaded historian Futrell that employing strategic bombers in visual attacks on ground targets of opportunity was 'novel', but 'wasteful'. In many cases, Superfortresses were unloading bombs from 10,000 ft using nothing more than verbal instructions from a soldier on the ground with a radio.

On 30 July some 47 Superfortresses flew the 'Nannie Able' mission against the Chosen Nitrogen Explosives Factory in Hungnam, on the east coast of North Korea. Cloud cover forced at least some of the crews to bomb using APQ-13 radar, but the large fires set in the centre of the factory burned some of the clouds away, and the trailing B-29s got visual assistance for their radar bombing. All ordnance fell into the target area, destroying 30 per cent of the factory and badly damaging a further 40 per cent. The radar bombing was deemed 'superior', and was said to attest to the value of intensive radar training programmes within SAC.

A 'Nannie Baker' mission planned for 1 August (46 B-29s) was largely stymied by bad weather, although crews reported that the explosions of their bombs actually shook their aircraft at 16,000 ft. 'Nannie Charlie', against the Bogun Chemical Plant, on 3 August (39 B-29s) was apparently successful. The three 'Nannie' raids all went after plants that were clustered in Hungnam, and were viewed as handing the North Koreans a considerable setback.

On 4 August approval was officially given for B-29 attacks against strategic targets in North Korea. This effort became known as Interdiction Campaign No 1. Superfortress crews began an attempt to systematically destroy North Korea's supply lines and transportation routes. In addition, because MacArthur was interested in rolling stock and supplies that had accumulated in Seoul's marshalling yards, O'Donnell sent the 19th BG to the occupied South Korean capital on 4 August. He followed this up by sending the 22nd and 92nd BGs to the same target the following day. Once bomb damage assessment was made, O'Donnell's command announced that Seoul's transportation facilities would be 'inoperative for a considerable period of time'.

Between 4 and 10 August, the B-29s hit railroad marshalling yards in North Korea in an attempt to disrupt supplies, but the results were poor.

Perhaps the most under-appreciated mission in the US Air Force has been – and still is – weather reconnaissance. No military campaign would be able to proceed without it, yet its significance is often overlooked. Two weather reconnaissance squadrons (the 54th WRS at Guam and 512th WRS in Japan) operated WB-29s on weather flights. This WB-29B, its mission connoted by the box-shaped sensor package in the dorsal area, is aircraft 44-61734 of the 54th WRS (*US Air Force*)

Some 47 aircraft hit the Chosen Nitrogen Explosives Plant at Konan and 39 B-29s attacked the Bogun Chemical Plant.

SAC BOMB GROUP

The newly-arrived 307th BG flew its first mission against Pyongyang's marshalling yards on 8 August. Two days later, a major effort by the 22nd, 92nd and 98th BGs struck the marshalling yards and refinery at the North Korean port of Wonsan.

Having cleared away the accumulations of supplies at North Korea's main transportation hubs, Bomber Command now turned toward the bridges in the north. Between 12 and 20 August, a series of strategic road and rail bridges were attacked and destroyed, the B-29 crews adopting new combat techniques during these raids. The aircraft of the 22nd and 92nd BGs were fitted with racks for 500-lb bombs only, which were not considered big enough to do the job against strongly constructed bridges. Still, after hitting some targets several times, Superfortress crews were credited with having destroyed 37 of the 44 bridges targeted by the end of August, with the remaining seven being so badly damaged that they were unusable.

Yet despite this success, on the ground North Korean forces were on the verge of pushing the United Nations' allies into the sea. In Tokyo, MacArthur and his subordinates were unable to assemble anything resembling an integrated air campaign. The Navy assigned targets to carrier groups at sea, while Stratemeyer and O'Donnell went to a Target Selection Committee every time they wanted to make a change.

Without anyone from the Navy even participating in the plan, O'Donnell's command launched a B-29 carpet-bombing campaign against enemy troop concentrations in mid-August 1950. Initially stymied by weather, the FEAF Bomber Command formation got aloft on the 16th, when 98 Superfortresses assaulted frontline troops with 3084 500-lb and 150 1000-lb bombs. The biggest employment of airpower in direct support of ground forces since the Normandy invasion, the strike had a blast effect equivalent to 30,000 rounds of heavy artillery.

Air Force leaders apparently felt that this concentration of destructive power had little effect on enemy troops. After failing to come up with measurable bomb damage results, Stratemeyer recommended that future carpet-bombing by B-29s should be undertaken under two conditions only – as a desperation measure against identified and definite concentrations of hostile troops who were preparing to assault friendly forces, or against a limited area through which friendly troops would effect a penetration into enemy territory. In short, the value of the Superfortress as a troop support weapon was unproven.

Attempts to use B-29s for the same purpose the following month – in part because MacArthur, who never had a good grasp of air operations, suggested it – also produced ambiguous results.

TARGETS IN SEOUL

Despite success against bridges in North Korea, B-29 crews faced challenges striking targets around occupied Seoul. Historian Futrell described one of them;

'Of all the bridge targets assigned to FEAF Bomber Command, none was so perverse as the steel cantilever west railway bridge at Seoul, called by aircrews the "elastic bridge" because of its stubborn refusal to fall. Only the 19th BG possessed bomb racks fitting 2000-lb bombs, and it accordingly drew the task of destroying this rail bridge. Day after day, for nearly four weeks, the 19th BG hammered the bridge with 1000-, 2000- and 4000-lb general-purpose bombs. Blueprints were obtained from the Japanese who had built the bridge, fuse settings were varied to obtain damage to the superstructure as well as the abutments, but despite numerous hits that forced the communists to keep the decking under constant repair, the steel spans of the bridge still stood.

'So important was the destruction of the bridge that Gen MacArthur offered to command the air unit that dropped it, and Gen Stratemeyer privately promised a case of Scotch whiskey to the crew who would take it down.

'Shortly after the noon hour on 19 August, nine B-29s of the 19th BG trailed in over Seoul to place 54 tons of 1000-lb bombs on the west railway bridge. The bomber crews reported numerous hits – so many in fact that they thought they could surely finish off the weakened bridge the following day.

'Navy pilots of Task Force 77 had already made two attacks against the railway bridge, and at mid-afternoon on 19 August, the (aircraft carriers) *Philippine Sea* and *Valley Forge* launched 37 Corsairs and Skyraiders against this target. These dive-bombers scored eight hits, after which one of their number flew the length of the span at low level and reported that the bridge was still standing, but unusable for the foreseeable future.

'On 20 August the 19th BG returned to the Seoul railway bridge, but the crews found that two spans of the weakened structure were in the water. These spans had evidently collapsed some time during the night.

When this bomb-drop photograph was released, its public information caption described how these Superfortresses were 'bringing the war home to the communist hordes'. The myth that the enemy were mindless cattle persisted long after seasoned infantrymen of the Chinese Peoples Volunteers acquitted themselves well against the US Army and US Marines. The 'square H' on the tail is the identifier for the 98th BG, which came to Yokota, near Tokyo, in August 1950, and remained in the combat zone throughout the war. The most prominent aircraft seen in this photograph is Wichita-built B-29 45-21721 *TAIL WIND*, assigned to the 98th BG's 344th BS (*US Air Force*)

B-29 units employed a standard tarpaulin bag to protect the bomber's jutting nose wheel from the elements. Individual aircraft markings varied in the early years of the USAF, as this shot clearly shows. The Superfortress in the foreground (Martin-built B-29 44-27302) features the prominent 'buzz number' BF-302, such a marking system initially being adopted by the AAF soon after World War 2. These numbers were applied as quick identifiers, which could, among other things, enable irate citizens to report which aircraft had 'buzzed' them at low level. The numbers were used routinely during the Korean War by fighters and by B-26 Invaders, but their appearance on B-29 Superfortresses was inconsistent. The partially black-garbed, and numberless, 'Superfort' in the background is more typical of the Korean era than mission-marked BF-302 (*Norman Taylor*)

The B-29 crews bombed the bridge as directed, and this attack chopped down a third span of the structure. Gen MacArthur presented a trophy to both the 19th BG and to Navy Air Group 11 for their participation in the destruction of the west railway bridge at Seoul, and Gen Stratemeyer provided a case of Scotch for each group.'

In all, five major industrial centres in North Korea were earmarked for attack. This was the mission the Superfortress had been designed for, and by early September all known industrial facilities in North Korea had been destroyed except for some oil storage tanks at Rashin, which was perilously close to the Soviet border. A 22 August strike on Rashin by 64 B-29s was diverted by bad weather to secondary targets at Chongjin. Immediately thereafter, because of Rashin's proximity to the USSR, it was put off limits as a target – a policy that changed later.

On the night of 30 August a B-29 crew flew an experimental flare mission, illuminating a target bridge near Seoul for attack by B-26 Invaders. The B-29 apparently functioned perfectly well as a flare ship, and this job was later handled by Navy PB4Y-2 Privateers.

INCHON INVASION

By the end of August 1950, North Korean troops were within a few dozen miles of pushing MacArthur's UN forces into the sea. The dogged defence of the 'Pusan perimeter' prevented that from happening, but MacArthur had bigger plans. He hoped to reverse the tide of war with an amphibious invasion at Inchon, the port city on the Yellow Sea just west of Seoul. Operation *Chromite* would open a second front, divide North Korean forces and put friendly troops within a short distance of recapturing Seoul.

On 9 September Superfortress 44-62084 was hit by ground fire near Wolbong-ni and blew apart in mid-air. Usually the loss of an aircraft did not occur with such stunning swiftness. After all, a B-29 was like a huge living creature, with hydraulic and electrical arteries and veins, and numerous body parts, some more resistant to damage than others.

The stressed, pressurised hull of a Superfortress was 99 ft in length, and the aircraft had a wingspan of 29 ft 7 in and a wing area of no less than 1736 square feet. Its broad tail fin gave the bomber a height of 29 ft 7 in when measured to the tip from the ground. Even when empty, a Superfortress tipped the scales at 70,140 lbs. When fully loaded for take-off, it could weigh 124,000 lbs. The B-29 was really two distinct creatures, with a fore and aft, joined by a narrow and claustrophobic tunnel above the bomb-bay. It was small wonder that 'Super' was part of the name of the aircraft – a big, complex assemblage of machinery that was not difficult to see, or to hit with gunfire, but was very difficult to destroy.

Rarely was destruction so instantaneous as with aircraft 44-62084 of the 325th BS/92nd BG, which was a B-29A-60-BN model. As crewmembers were blown from the aircraft like confetti in a windstorm, five parachutes were observed to open. In later years, however, only two of those aboard (S/Sgts Arthur W Hoult and James H Duncan) would emerge from PoW camps in the north. The remains of one other crew member (Capt Zane M Hoit) were recovered decades later, but the fate of the remaining eight crewmen has never been determined.

On 14 September the Inchon landing took place. Within hours MacArthur's troops had seized Kimpo airfield and, within days, Seoul. For a time there was discussion about the Korean War being over. Most North Korean troops had now been chased back from whence they had come – the north side of the 38th Parallel. But MacArthur wanted to go after them and wipe them out once and for all.

Eight B-29s of the 92nd BG returned to the North Korean harbour city of Hungnam on 26 September to attack its hydroelectric plant. US leaders were still attempting to decide whether to move into North Korea and, if so, whether to bomb targets that were part of its infrastructure.

The following day MacArthur won approval to advance into North Korea. His forces crossed the 38th Parallel on 1 October, and Pyongyang fell 18 days later. Having completely reversed the tide of war, enthusiastic American soldiers and Marines, together with troops from 16 Allied countries, advanced rapidly toward the Yalu River. During this period, many B-29s were diverted to tactical strikes, since strategic bombing was no longer necessary because most of North Korea was now in Allied hands. But the JCS in the Pentagon threw cold water on a plan by Stratemeyer – approved by MacArthur – to use 100 B-29s with demolition bombs against targets in the North Korean capital, Pyongyang. Bombing raids on Pyongyang were flown, but the plan for a mass attack was nixed.

Throughout the Korean War, from the first day to the last, official UN policy was against crossing the border into Manchuria (China) to attack forces that might support the now-exhausted North Koreans. In the autumn of 1950, swept-wing jet fighters began to appear at airfields along the Yalu River on the protected Manchurian side. Most in the West, including intelligence experts, had not yet heard the term 'MiG-15', but that would soon change. Meanwhile, when a B-29 crew of the 98th BG made a navigational error, crossed the river, and bombed the Antung marshalling yard in Manchuria on 22 September 1950, Stratemeyer and O'Donnell chastised the crew and instituted tighter briefing procedures.

MIXED MISSIONS

While some B-29 crews continued to fly night flare missions (gradually developing a 'buddy' system which saw one Superfortress drop M26 flares while another aimed on the illumination with its bombs) over North Korea, others continued to support UN troops by daylight. Strate-

What they looked like when they came home. Returning to March Air Force Base, California, from the Korean War zone in late 1950, this Superfortress crew displays the spit and polish that was sometimes missing during the war, but ever-present in Strategic Air Command. Apparently lined up for inspection, the men wear a curious mixture of ball caps and neckties, line badges and low-quarter shoes. This particular crew fought with the 92nd BG early in the Korean War, but crews who fought as late as July 1953 also returned home to face SAC's strict rules on decorum (*Carl Miller*)

meyer scheduled 12 B-29s for continuous surveillance over the main roads leading from the frontlines toward Seoul, which was now in friendly hands. The object was to bomb retreating North Korean army units, but the success of these missions was hard to quantify.

In the immediate aftermath of the Inchon landing, Stratemeyer sent 13 B-29s to bombard the retreating North Korean troops with psychological warfare leaflets that urged them to surrender. For generations, foreign-policy experts have argued that propaganda leaflets don't work, but then – as now – military leaders were impervious to this criticism. And as if to prove their point, on 27 September a group of 104 North Koreans clutching the leaflets actually surrendered to American soldiers, thus bringing a modest success to a method that usually achieves none.

27 September also saw the JCS decide that the North Korean army was defeated, and they cancelled all further strategic air attacks against North Korean objectives. All air operations were now supposed to be diverted toward tactical targets.

The rapid northward thrust of friendly troops made it more difficult for FEAF Bomber Command to carry out a campaign against bridges in North Korea. On 6 October FEAF sent the command a list of 33 bridges that were to be dropped north of Pyongyang and Wonsan. The destruction of the spans would isolate hostile troops in North Korea's two principal cities. However, South Korean troops advanced so rapidly up the east coast that the command was forced to delete ten of the bridges from its target roster. The list had to be revised a second time when the Eighth Army reached a point far north of Wonsan in late October. By then, for sheer lack of targets, FEAF's deputy commander, Gen O P Weyland, had ordered Bomber Command to decrease its sorties by 25 per cent.

As historian Futrell wrote, 'Finding nothing better to bomb, one 92nd BG crew recorded that it chased an enemy soldier on a motorcycle down a road, dropping bombs until one hit the hapless fellow'.

By the end of October, MacArthur authorised Stratemeyer to release the 22nd and 92nd BGs for return to the United States. Many of their aircraft remained in the combat zone and were transferred.

ENEMY FIGHTERS

On 18 October an RB-29 reconnaissance crew of the 31st SRS peered across the Yalu River and counted more than 75 fighters parked in neat rows at Antung airfield. We know today that these were MiG-15s belonging to a Soviet fighter regiment. The fighters were gone the following day, and Stratemeyer concluded that the enemy had merely displayed the aircraft as 'window dressing'. The general was about to learn, however, that the MiG threat was very real.

Gene Fisher, the 30th BS/19th BG gunner who had previously been shot up by a Yak-9, was still a crewmember on *Bug's Ball Buster* when the MiGs began to appear. The following account by Fisher is to some extent at variance with other recollections;

'The first time I spotted a MiG-15 was on the 23 October 1950 mission – a seven-and-a-half-hour marathon – to the bridges along the Yalu River. We could see the Manchurian air bases on the other side of the border (the Yalu River). We could see the MiGs taking off. When they made passes at us I could see their noses lighting up, which has to mean they were shooting at us with their cannons. We fired back, but apparently neither of us hit the other.'

Fisher eventually finished 61 combat missions, mostly in daylight, with only one abort, and was awarded five air medals;

'That was one scary place along the Manchurian border, and it was even scarier for us because we were afraid they were going to ask us to bomb China. We had begun the Korean War with only a handful of B-29s, and I wondered how the hell were we going to bomb China?'

And although some people were talking about the war ending and the troops coming home, Fisher wasn't hearing any of it.

Near the end of October 1950, American soldiers stood on the Yalu and looked across the river into Manchuria. *The Washington Daily News* published a cover photograph of a wounded US soldier, and began its caption with, 'Now that the Korean War is almost over . . .'. MacArthur is widely understood to have predicted that American troops would be home for Christmas, although efforts to pin down the quote were not successful. Some units held 'victory parties'. The sense that a short, miserable war would soon be over permeated UN military units everywhere.

The coming victory seemed so certain that the 22nd and 92nd BWs were sent home to resume their SAC duties. The move was affirmation that the United States continued to give higher priority to confronting the Soviet Union than to fighting North Koreans. As for the Chinese, who were now nudged up against the Yalu within eyesight of American forces, no one in Washington seemed to be thinking about them.

Then, on 1 November, F-51 Mustangs were engaged by six swept-wing jet fighters from across the Yalu. The river remained a forbidden boundary for the Americans. Intelligence experts saw huge, modern airfields on the Chinese side, but knew little of what was happening in China, or about the swept-wing jets that were now being reported.

The top brass continued to believe that the war was ending. They saw no prospect of China intervening on the ground, and attached little significance to those MiGs in the air. When Lt Col Clure Smith, an F-80C Shooting Star squadron commander, came back from a mission

Its nose covered in mission markings (painted as camera silhouettes), 44-61817 was another Renton-built RB-29A that saw extensive service in Korea with the 91st SRS in the early months of the war (*Mike Moffitt*)

with a gun-camera photo of a MiG-15 limping north across the Yalu trailing smoke, no one seemed terribly interested. Like the king who wore no garments, the MiG-15 could be seen by the likes of Smith, but remained invisible to those unwilling to open their eyes.

While the signs were growing that the war might not be ending as soon as everyone believed, bomber crews were being given orders for a final campaign that would break the back of North Korean resistance. On 5 November MacArthur ordered two weeks of maximum air efforts. This included an order to destroy Yalu bridges on the Korean side. That day, 21 B-29s of the 19th BG came upon excellent weather over their secondary target, Kanggye, and dropped 170 tons of incendiaries – the first use of firebombs in the Korean War.

MacArthur's sweeping air campaign order lasted only a day, for on 6 November, sensitive about provoking an incident with China, the JCS, on direction from President Truman himself, ordered MacArthur to postpone any bombing attacks within five miles of the Chinese border. MacArthur replied that men and materiel were pouring across the Yalu bridges. The JCS reversed their order to halt all strikes, but emphasised that MacArthur's aircraft were not to cross the border.

What UN experts did not know, and most of us did not learn until years later, was than the 'Chinese air force' consisted of entire regiments of Russians who were drilling in MiG-15s on the north bank of the Yalu. It was bad enough (as we shall see) that MacArthur's staff was unaware of the surprise the Chinese were cooking up. Nearly as bad was the fact that the Allies had no idea so many Russians were flying jet fighters just across the border. On rare occasion when the they heard the Russian language in the enemy's VHF (very high frequency) radio transmissions, the bland assumption was made that a very few Russian advisors were helping out up there.

In fact, the MiG-15s were available in significant numbers and, in the beginning at least, only Russian pilots were permitted to fly combat sorties in the new communist fighter. And in due time, they would constitute a threat to the B-29 force of incredible proportions.

SINUIJU

Historian Robert F Futrell wrote of the dilemma of B-29 crews trying to bomb bridges without crossing the Yalu, and trying to attack targets that were on-again, off-again for the JCS;

'Although Gen Stratemeyer had scheduled all-out strikes against Sinuiju before receiving MacArthur's air-campaign directive, the city of Sinuiju was the foremost of the type of targets which MacArthur wished FEAF would go and attack. It lay on the southern shore of the Yalu, directly across the river from the Manchurian city of Antung (the site of the enemy's biggest MiG base). Two three-quarter-mile-long bridges connected the two cities – one was a combination rail and highway bridge, the other a double-track railway bridge. The city itself was the seat of Kim Il-sung's fugitive government, and its warehouses and dwellings quite possibly sheltered communist troops and supplies.

'Weather prevented the all-out attack planned for 7 November, but on the following day the Fifth Air Force and FEAF Bomber Command executed maximum-strength strikes against Sinuiju. Before the B-29s arrived, Fifth Air Force F-80 jets and F-51 fighters raked hostile anti-aircraft artillery positions with machine guns, rockets and napalm. As the fighter-bombers were suppressing flak, MiG-15s came up from Antung to engage top-cover (F-80) flights which were flown by 51st Fighter Interceptor Wing pilots.'

One of those pilots was 1Lt Russell J Brown, who was credited with shooting down a MiG-15 in an aerial duel along the Yalu. Today, Russian records indicate that no MiG was lost on that date, but Brown retains credit as the victor in history's first jet-versus-jet battle.

Futrell continues:

'Shortly before noon, 70 B-29s came over Sinuiju to drop 584.5 tons of 500-lb incendiary clusters. Under the cover of this assault, nine other B-29s dropped 1000-lb bombs upon the abutments and approaches of the two international bridges. As the B-29s came over, communist flak batteries from the Manchurian side of the river threw up a heavy volume of fire, but the bombers held altitudes above 18,000 ft and flew in squadrons in close trail, clearing the target in the shortest possible time. The MiGs did not appear and the flak did no damage. Comparison of photographs taken before and after the holocaust revealed that the incendiary bombs had burned out 60 per cent of the two-square-mile, built-up area of Sinuiju. But the spans of the two international bridges were still standing – the 19th BG's B-29s had damaged the approaches to the bridges, but they had not closed the structures to communist traffic.'

In the aftermath of this huge raid, American officers apparently exaggerated the results of their effort – as, indeed, both sides did throughout the war. In *The Forgotten War*, Clay Blair wrote;

'Ironically, this much debated, politically sensitive attack failed – not one bomb hit the bridges. Follow-up attacks the next day by carrier-based naval dive-bombers knocked out one span on the Korean end of the highway bridge, but repeated attacks by FEAF and Navy aeroplanes failed to knock out the other bridges. A fortnight later, when the Yalu River at Sinuiju froze over, the surviving two bridges lost their importance.'

The following day (9 November) MiGs shot up a 31st SRS RB-29 and sent it back to crash-land (with the loss of five crewmen) at Johnson Air Base, in Japan. In that action, the RB-29's tail gunner, Cpl Harry J LaVene, was credited with having shot down a MiG-15. It was apparently the first loss of a reconnaissance Superfortress in combat.

On 16 November the 91st SRS absorbed the 31st, the loss of a bomber having blunted the squadron's effectiveness – FEAF now forbade the RB-29s from approaching the Yalu, sending RF-80As to reconnoitre the river instead. At this juncture, the 91st SRS consisted of nine RB-29s, including three equipped with SHORAN (Short Range Navigation) gear and two modified for 'ferret' or radar reconnaissance missions.

Just 24 hours after the 31st SRS RB-29 was shot up, MiG-15s destroyed a 307th BG B-29 near the Yalu. Three more Superfortresses were damaged by cannon fire from MiGs over the next two weeks. An intelligence report released at this time stated that Chinese pilots flew the MiGs, and that China had no intention of becoming more deeply involved in the war. Both assertions were false.

Also built at Renton, RB-29A Superfortress 44-61949 of the 91st SRS is marked with the unit's distinctive 'circle X' tail marking. It was photographed at an unnamed airfield in Korea after diverting following a mission 'up north' in late 1950. The aircraft wears a Fifteenth Air Force patch on the lower forward segment of its fin, indicating its connection to SAC and to the 91st's former home at McGuire Field, New Jersey. Silhouettes of cameras appear on the nose as mission markers (*Mike Moffitt*)

When groundcrew and aircrew were working together to 'prep' a B-29 for a mission, it was like a choreographed performance. This RB-29A Superfortress (44-61727) of the 91st SRS wears a name derived from its serial, *SEVEN TO SEVEN*, plus the words *"SO TIRED"*, and a scantily-clad maiden designed to discourage the viewer from thinking about sleep (*Mike Moffitt*)

Between 9 and 25 November, Superfortresses and naval air power continued to assault bridges, marshalling yards and supply centres in the tiny portion of North Korea that remained in the enemy's hands. On one mission, the 98th BG sent nine B-29s to 'walk' 1000-lb bombs across the Sinuiju bridges. On another, the 19th and 307th BGs teamed up to attack the same bridges. In one encounter, MiGs seriously damaged two B-29s, and yet the Allies continued to conduct themselves as if the MiG threat did not exist.

As incredible as it seems, no one in the west had taken it seriously when Chinese Premier Chou En-lai had warned in a speech that China would send troops into Korea if the Allies advanced north of the 38th Parallel. In a stunning move, China inserted half a million troops into North Korea. Allied intelligence experts were asleep at the switch.

The Chinese came swarming into the midst of UN troops without the support of a heavy artillery barrage, the communists instead relying on the sheer weight of numbers associated with a full-scale frontal assault. Indeed, they relied primarily on their long, thin bayonets to carry the day, prevailing in bitter hand-to-hand combat before any western official would even say that China was in the war!

Yes, American soldiers had captured a handful of Chinese 'volunteers' as early as mid-November. But now, the UN forces faced no fewer than 50 Chinese divisions. In the air, the MiG-15 seemed on the verge of wresting air supremacy over the Korean peninsula and bushwhacking American B-29s with ease. For the remainder of the war, the allies' taboo on crossing the Yalu into China was to give the Chinese air force, and its Chinese and Russian pilots, an enormous advantage.

The Chinese attacked with incredible boldness on the ground. Commanded by Marshal Peng Te-huai (not, as is widely written, by Marshal Lin Piao), the Chinese Peoples Volunteers were tough battle veterans who'd seized all of mainland China from Chiang Kai-shek's armies the year before. Peng himself, with a headquarters in Mukden,

Yet another Renton-built RB-29A, 44-61854 of the 91st SRS was photographed soon after its arrival in the Far East. It does not yet feature the unit's distinctive squadron markings (*Mike Moffitt*)

100 miles north of the Yalu, was a seasoned veteran of guerrilla fighting in South China, as well as of Mao Tse-tung's famous Long March and later struggles against Chiang.

In the west, the press conjured up images of Chinese soldiers rushing into battle, shoulder to shoulder, in massed 'human wave' attacks. Some reports made the Chinese infantryman an unthinking, dope-crazed fanatic bent on suicide.

The Chinese made little use of heavy artillery and armour. They launched ground attacks with enormous numbers of men, sometimes to the blare of bugles, but these were capable soldiers, not mindless fanatics. Had the Chinese possessed true air power, and had the Allies not controlled the skies, the intervention of China into the war might have enabled the foe to seize all of the Korean peninsula.

On the American home front, the Chinese attack was the most devastating blow to the public since Pearl Harbor. On 25 November Chinese troops intervened massively in the war, rapidly pushing their UN counterparts back below the 38th Parallel. Any chance for the forced reunification of Korea had been lost. The B-29s flew close support missions in an attempt to slow the Chinese advance, and it was not until the end of December that the line stabilised. However, the daylight bombing flights, which had been unopposed during the first months of the war, now faced flak and aerial opposition. Lavochkin La-7 and La-9 and Yakovlev Yak-9P fighters, and the increasingly ubiquitous MiG-15s, seemed to be everywhere.

The B-29 effort against the Yalu bridges was stymied by terrible weather at the end of November 1950. MacArthur began to doubt the wisdom of sending B-29s all the way up to the border with so many enemy fighters flying around. He was frustrated, also, by evidence that although B-29s had been extremely successful against communications and supply targets, they had fared less well when sent against industrial centres and troop concentrations. Moreover, the campaign against the Yalu bridges came too late to matter – by the time B-29 crews dropped some of the spans, the bulk of the attacking Chinese troops were already inside North Korea.

On 15 November, perhaps in testimony to the belief by many that the Superfortress was underpowered on take-off, a B-29 attempted to abort after starting its take-off roll at Kadena, It crashed at the end of the runway, causing the bomber to burst into flames. As two firefighters entered the aircraft to attempt to save a crewmember, the Superfortress exploded, killing all three. The aircraft was B-29-50-MO 44-86328, which had been manufactured in Omaha, Nebraska, by the Glenn L Martin Company. It belonged to the 28th BS/19th BG. As firefighter Bob Crevisour remembered years later;

'When the crashed B-29 exploded at the China Sea end of the strip, it demolished our crash equipment and blew the station apart, along with the control tower. The bomber's aircraft commander 1Lt Charlie R Smith. Radio operator James P Cooper was killed, as well as firefighters S/Sgt Richard D Patterson and Cpl Jack Morris.'

Several firefighting vehicles were also severely damaged in the crash. The loss of Patterson and Morris was a grim reminder that war extracted a cost from many USAF personnel, not just aircrew.

NEW WAR

On 28 November MacArthur reported to his superiors that he was being assaulted by 200,000 Chinese troops, which were overrunning Allied positions everywhere. The war that had seemed finished just weeks earlier was now becoming a defeat, and then a rout. MacArthur would later claim that the enemy succeeded because the Allies were not permitted to bomb on the far side of the Yalu. One of his contingency plans called for using tactical atomic bombs (not yet generally called nuclear weapons) on both sides of the river. Had the plan materialised, B-29s would have carried the era's 'Fat Man' plutonium bombs, which were improved versions of the weapon that had devastated Nagasaki five years earlier. The B-29s in the combat theatre were not modified for that purpose, and crews were not trained for it.

The arrival of the 4th Fighter Interceptor Group, with its Sabres, was good news for beleaguered B-29 crews. But on the ground, UN troops were falling back and fighting harsh winter conditions as much as the enemy. Efforts to provide air support to the Marines at the Chosin Reservoir could not prevent their being forced to withdraw to the Hungnam-Hamhung perimeter on the east coast, where they were evacuated by sea.

On 4 and 5 December, B-29s repeatedly bombed several North Korean marshalling centres in an effort to slow the enemy's advance. It soon became clear that MacArthur's armies would have to retreat from the North Korean capital, and on 10 December B-29s potholed the two airfields at Pyongyang with high-explosive bombs.

Four days later, the 19th BG bombed Pyongyang's rail yards and nearby storage areas, seeking to destroy abandoned US equipment. B-29s also ranged over North Korea striking other targets. Just before Christmas, the Superfortress campaign shifted its attention to towns and villages suspected of harbouring hostile troops.

Members of the 345th BS/98th BG at Yokota prepare to board a B-29 for a combat mission on Christmas Eve 1950 (*Jess Richey*)

1951

For the second time since the Korean War had started, the Allies were losing. When they weren't flying, B-29 Superfortress crewmembers listened to Armed Forces Radio or read the *Stars & Stripes* newspaper, and encountered nothing but bad news.

The UN Command forces under the leadership of Gen Douglas MacArthur began the second calendar year of the conflict reeling, licking wounds and falling back. At the start of January 1951, Chinese troops were on the outskirts of Seoul, and were coming through the wire at the city's nearby K-14 Kimpo airfield. They quickly took the South Korean capital, which had already changed hands twice.

Allied intelligence experts tried to analyse the enemy's aerial threat. Unlike the United States, which had no jet bombers in the region (except for three RB-45C Tornado reconnaissance aircraft at Yokota, one of which was shot down by a MiG-15 shortly after its arrival), the Soviet Union and the Chinese had Ilyushin Il-28s in the region. Their presence caused some experts to worry that the Chinese might attempt to bomb the two B-29 Superfortress groups stationed on Okinawa.

The threat of offensive action by enemy air power was to persist throughout the war. It had an impact on every aspect of planning, yet the dreaded air strikes by enemy aeroplanes never came. For whatever reason, the foe elected not to use airpower as an offensive striking weapon.

CREW LIFE

For the crews of the B-29, it was no easy proposition to climb into a steel cocoon, strap down and prepare to travel into harm's way. In his memoir of life as a navigator with the 344th BS/98th BG, former 1Lt Vernon R 'Bob' Hudder described a routine that seemed almost like drudgery, experienced by men who had to be in a constant state of anxiety;

'Every morning, we were required to check the squadron bulletin board to see if we were scheduled for the next mission. If we were on the list, we would report to the mission briefing room at the scheduled time and sit in the row assigned to our crew.

'The room was fairly large, and on the front wall was a large map of Korea that was covered when the briefing began. The group commander usually conducted the briefings, and prior to his drawing back the black curtain that covered the map, there was much suspense. Would it be a "hot" target or a "milk run"? Red ribbons placed on the map showed the target and approaches. Briefings were never dull! After the briefings,

The resourcefulness of nose art specialists was unrelenting. *"SNOOPY DROOPY"*, believed to be a B-29 of the 344th BS/98th BG, drew its canine caricature from a popular children's cartoon of the early 1950s (*Roland T Speckman*)

the chaplains had rooms where crews could go for a time of prayer before preparation for the mission.

'Sometime prior to taking off, our crew would report to the B-29 for aircraft inspection, and to fuse the bombs. On several occasions, we had to sweep snow off the wings.

'Near our scheduled take-off time, our crew lined up to be inspected by the Aircraft Commander. Our parachutes were laid on the tarmac in front of each crewmember, and we wore our "Mae West" life preservers around our necks. We also carried a 0.45-cal pistol in a shoulder holster. In the many pockets of my flight suit, I crammed all kinds of survival type foods. After boarding the aircraft, we did not close the hatches until the chaplain came by to shake hands and give us his blessing.'

At times, they were going to need it.

An intelligence officer (centre, rear) debriefs a B-29 Superfortress crew from the 343rd BS/98th BG at Yokota after a combat mission. The first lieutenant is writing down the crew's account of what happened over the target. He will compare it with intelligence reports, and help the top brass to understand what has been learned about the enemy's defences, and the effectiveness of the mission (*US Air Force*)

TARGET PYONGYANG

On 3 January 1951, some 63 Superfortresses struck supply facilities and personnel concentrations in Pyongyang. One crewmember described the North Korean capital as 'millions of thatched-roof huts and dirt pathways that spilled into a central downtown area with factories, a parade ground and clusters of office buildings'. Two days later, 60 B-29s dropped incendiary bombs on the capital, only to have the effects of the firebombs partly thwarted by snow on the straw-covered rooftops. Still, according to historian Robert F Futrell, Radio Pyongyang responded to the attack by reporting that 'the entire city burned like a furnace for two whole days'.

There was intense air activity by tactical aeroplanes in North Korea. And although the MiG-15s had not yet concentrated on B-29 formations, crewmembers knew that the MiGs spelled danger on virtually every mission. As the year progressed, the number of MiGs in easy striking distance on the forbidden side of the Yalu soon reached 445.

A hint of what the jets might do to the B-29s came in late January when the fighters 'boxed' four F-80C Shooting Stars near Sinuiju and shot one of them down. For the MiG pilots, it was like shooting skeet in a trap. In the weeks that followed, planners kept B-29s away from the north-western region of North Korea, which had become dubbed 'MiG Alley', deeming it too dangerous for the Superfortress crews.

On 10 January an important command change took place. Gen Emmett 'Rosie' O'Donnell, who had led B-29 formations in combat in two wars, rotated back to the United States. Brig Gen James E Briggs became commander of FEAF Bomber Command, and MacArthur immediately asked him to increase B-29 pressure on Pyongyang.

Briggs decided to send B-29s back to 'MiG Alley' beginning on 1 March, the Bomber Command boss scheduling the 98th BG to make attacks in the region that day, escorted by 22 F-80Cs. The group's 18 B-29s ran into unexpected head winds, and were so late making the rendezvous that the Shooting Stars had to break off and return to base. This left the Superfortresses with no fighter escort when it came time to dropping their bombs. MiGs arrived and took them under attack.

In the fighting that ensued, a B-29 gunner was credited with downing a MiG-15. It needs to be added that a review board approved many such aerial victory claims on days when – as the opening up of Soviet records would later reveal – no MiG was lost. Moreover, the MiGs damaged ten of the bombers, three so badly that they had to make emergency landings in South Korea. It was a poignant reminder that 'MiG Alley' was a dangerous place, as well as a harbinger of worse problems to come.

Four weeks later, on 29 March, the 19th BG targeted the Yalu bridges with three 19th BG Superfortresses that were sent to Sinuiju equipped with Tarzon bombs. These machines seemed to be plagued by bad luck, for one of the B-29s aborted with mechanical problems and another, piloted by 19th BG commander Col Payne Jennings, apparently ditched at sea with the loss of all on board. The third B-29 reached Sinuiju but missed the target with its Tarzon.

Apparently the largest bomb used in Korea, the Tarzon was a big brother of the radio-controlled weapons known as VB-3 Razons that were dropped from B-29s against bridges in early 1951. After release from the Superfortress bomb-bay, they were guided to the target by the bombardier using a remote control unit. They were named Razon because the controller could alter RAnge and AZimuth ONly once they left the aircraft. The Razons were 1000-lb bombs, their relatively modest size enabling a single weapon to be easily accommodated within the forward bomb-bay of a B-29. Experts soon concluded, however, that the Razon was not heavy enough for the bridge-busting mission.

Considered a combination of the American Razon and the British Tallboy bomb, the Tarzon tipped the scales at a staggering 12,000 lbs, and was credited with a circular error of probability of about 280 ft. It was also known as the MX-674 and later the VB-13 (for 'vertical bomb'), and had been developed by Bell Aircraft. Unfortunately, the Tarzon had a size problem, being so colossal that more than half of the weapon protruded outside the bomb-bay, causing the potential for the B-29 to suffer from handling problems in flight due to excessive drag – the Tarzon was the primary suspect in the loss of the Jennings crew.

B-29s dropped 30 Tarzons in Korea, but only six bridges were severed. Jennings' and one other bomber were lost on Tarzon missions, apparently when trying to ditch their bombs into the sea. Within weeks of their introduction the Tarzons were withdrawn.

To B-29 crews, Soviet MiG-15 fighters over Korea were little more than blurs in motion – this photograph was snapped by a bomber crewman during one such high speed encounter. The Soviet pilots on the forbidden side of the Yalu River did not initially concentrate their efforts against the B-29 force, so it was not until the autumn of 1951 that the MiGs forced the bombers to abandon daylight raids (*US Air Force*)

A Superfortress releases 500-lb bombs over North Korea. This image was accompanied by a press release claiming that it depicts the 150th combat mission flown by the 19th BG in February 1951 (*US Air Force*)

On 30 March, during a welcome break in the cloudy weather, the 19th, 98th and 307th BGs sent a dozen Superfortresses each in the first major attack of the spring against the Yalu River bridges. Now, there were eight flights of F-86s patrolling high above the bombers, and their presence seemed to tell any potential foe that discretion was the better part of valour. Some MiGs came aloft, but none rose to the altitude of the Sabres.

The 19th BG formation was the only one that came under attack from MiGs, the enemy fighters swooping in and out of the bomber stream and firing cannon bursts that wounded one crewmember. Gunners aboard the Superfortresses were given credit for downing two MiG-15s. The mission had barely ended – with a B-29 pausing at Itazuke Air Base, near Fukuoka, Japan, to offload a wounded crewman – when the exasperating clouds so common to North Korea returned to cover the bridges, preventing a battle damage assessment and delaying further raids for a week.

A 31 March mission to a different highway bridge at Linchiang was disappointing to the crews of the 19th BG and to the FEAF brass. The mission was flown by relatively inexperienced crews and produced ambiguous results. Behind the scenes, officials continued to bicker over the selection and assignment of targets – an endeavour that was never handled well at any time in the conflict.

While the B-29s awaited better weather, the brass debated ways to improve fighter escort operations. There was doubt that efforts by MacArthur, Stratemeyer and Briggs to heighten the effectiveness of Superfortress raids were succeeding. One of those most concerned was SAC boss Gen Curtis E LeMay, who had sent Col Ashley B Packard's 27th Fighter Escort Wing (FEW), equipped with F-84E/G Thunderjets, to Korea. He urged that the unit be given escort assignments, and Gen Earle E Partridge, commander of FEAF's Fifth Air Force, duly removed the Itazuke-based 27th FEW from the air-to-ground mission schedule. The Thunderjets drew their first escort mission on 7 April, flying parallel to boxes of B-29s from the 98th and 307th BGs as they struck the newly-built highway bridge at Uiju and the railway bridge at Sinuiju.

Thirty MiG-15s challenged the B-29s, the accompanying F-84s and the screen of Sabres operating at higher altitude. Only a single MiG drew within firing range of the Superfortresses, but it so effectively raked a B-29 with cannon fire that the latter crashed behind enemy lines. The Thunderjets claimed a MiG in a fighter escort effort that won praise from Bomber Command boss Brig Gen James E Briggs.

The work of the bombers was another matter. Sinuiju's massive railway bridge was unscathed, so Briggs ordered the three B-29 groups – the 19th, 98th and 307th BGs – to pay it another visit. On 12 April, with Sabres as top cover and Thunderjets as direct escort, the Superfortresses again went after the bridge. Things got off to a shaky start when nine of the 48 B-29s aborted with mechanical and other problems (*text continues on page 49*).

Although of poor quality, this snap captures a particularly happy moment for S/Sgt Richard E 'Gene' Fisher of the 30th BS/19th BG. Taken on 5 April 1951, it shows Fisher (fourth from right) minutes after completing his 61st, and last, combat mission. Having served both as a left and tail gunner, Fisher flew the bulk of his sorties in B-29A-40-BN Superfortress 44-61638 *Bug's Ball Buster*, which provides the backdrop for this photograph (*Gene Fisher*)

COLOUR PLATES

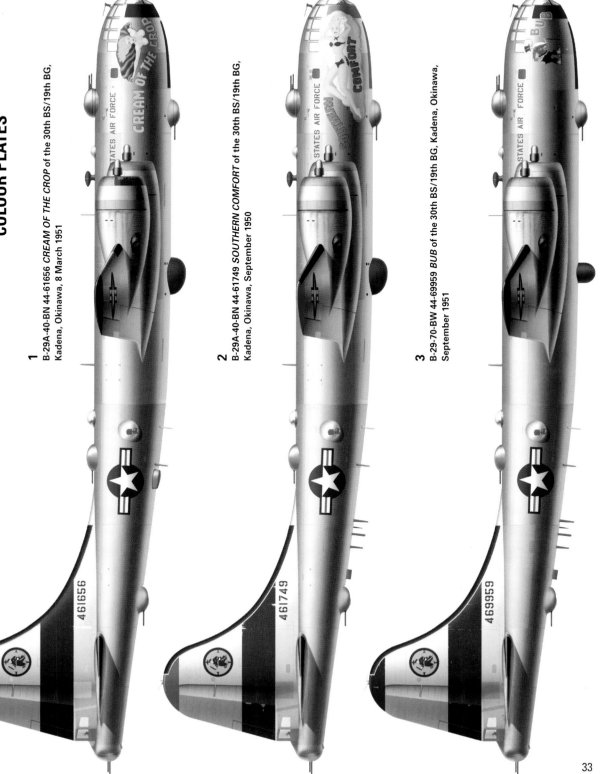

1
B-29A-40-BN 44-61656 *CREAM OF THE CROP* of the 30th BS/19th BG, Kadena, Okinawa, 8 March 1951

2
B-29A-40-BN 44-61749 *SOUTHERN COMFORT* of the 30th BS/19th BG, Kadena, Okinawa, September 1950

3
B-29-70-BW 44-69959 *BUB* of the 30th BS/19th BG, Kadena, Okinawa, September 1951

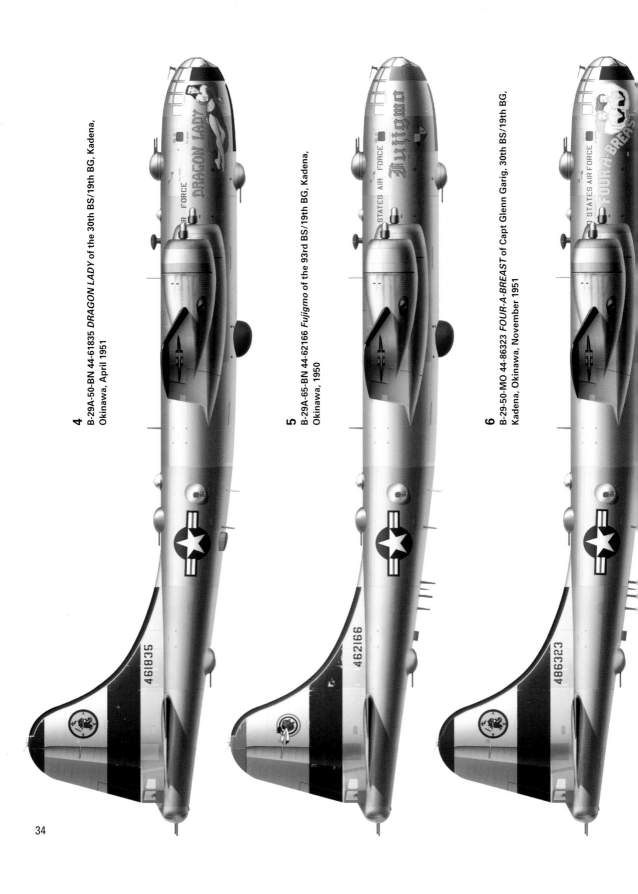

4
B-29A-50-BN 44-61835 *DRAGON LADY* of the 30th BS/19th BG, Kadena, Okinawa, April 1951

5
B-29A-65-BN 44-62166 *Fujigmo* of the 93rd BS/19th BG, Kadena, Okinawa, 1950

6
B-29-50-MO 44-86323 *FOUR-A-BREAST* of Capt Glenn Garig, 30th BS/19th BG, Kadena, Okinawa, November 1951

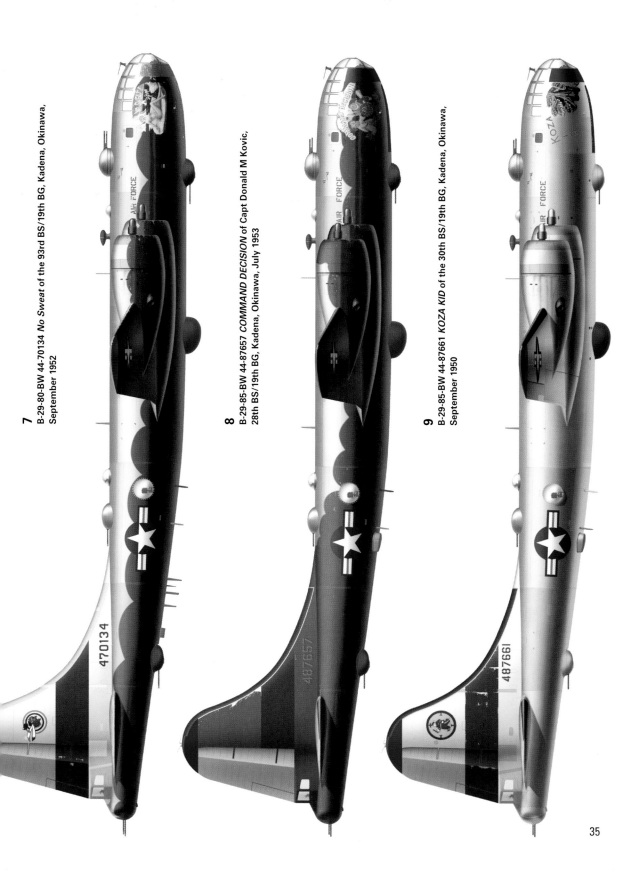

7

B-29-80-BW 44-70134 *No Sweat* of the 93rd BS/19th BG, Kadena, Okinawa,
September 1952

8

B-29-85-BW 44-87657 *COMMAND DECISION* of Capt Donald M Kovic,
28th BS/19th BG, Kadena, Okinawa, July 1953

9

B-29-85-BW 44-87661 *KOZA KID* of the 30th BS/19th BG, Kadena, Okinawa,
September 1950

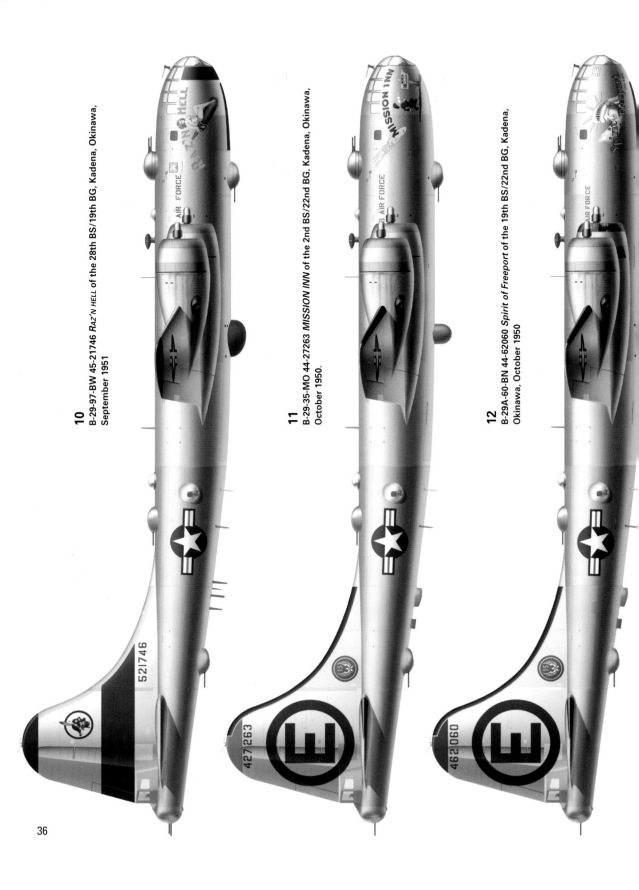

10
B-29-97-BW 45-21746 *RAZ'N HELL* of the 28th BS/19th BG, Kadena, Okinawa, September 1951

11
B-29-35-MO 44-27263 *MISSION INN* of the 2nd BS/22nd BG, Kadena, Okinawa, October 1950.

12
B-29A-60-BN 44-62060 *Spirit of Freeport* of the 19th BS/22nd BG, Kadena, Okinawa, October 1950

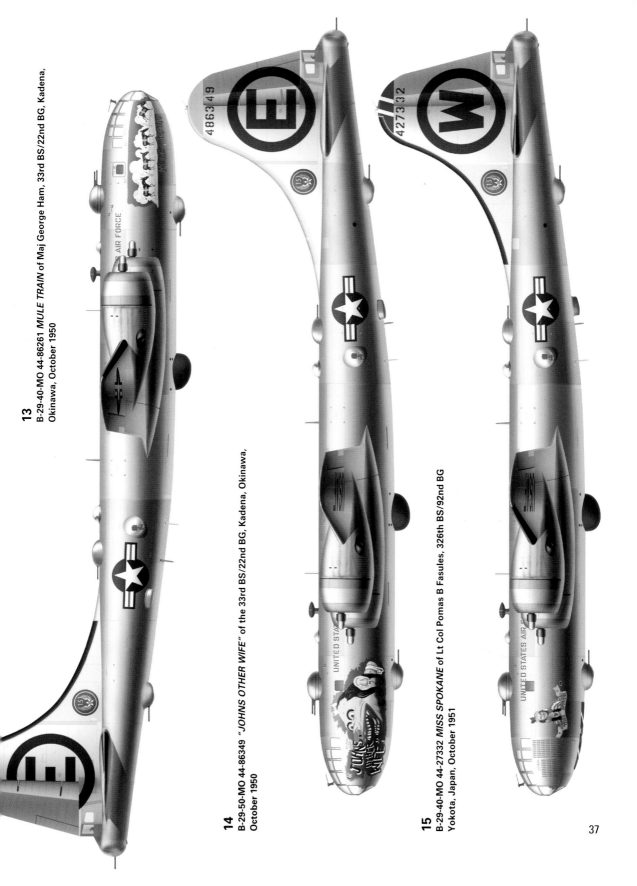

13
B-29-40-MO 44-86261 *MULE TRAIN* of Maj George Ham, 33rd BS/22nd BG, Kadena, Okinawa, October 1950

14
B-29-50-MO 44-86349 *"JOHNS OTHER WIFE"* of the 33rd BS/22nd BG, Kadena, Okinawa, October 1950

15
B-29-40-MO 44-27332 *MISS SPOKANE* of Lt Col Pomas B Fasules, 326th BS/92nd BG Yokota, Japan, October 1951

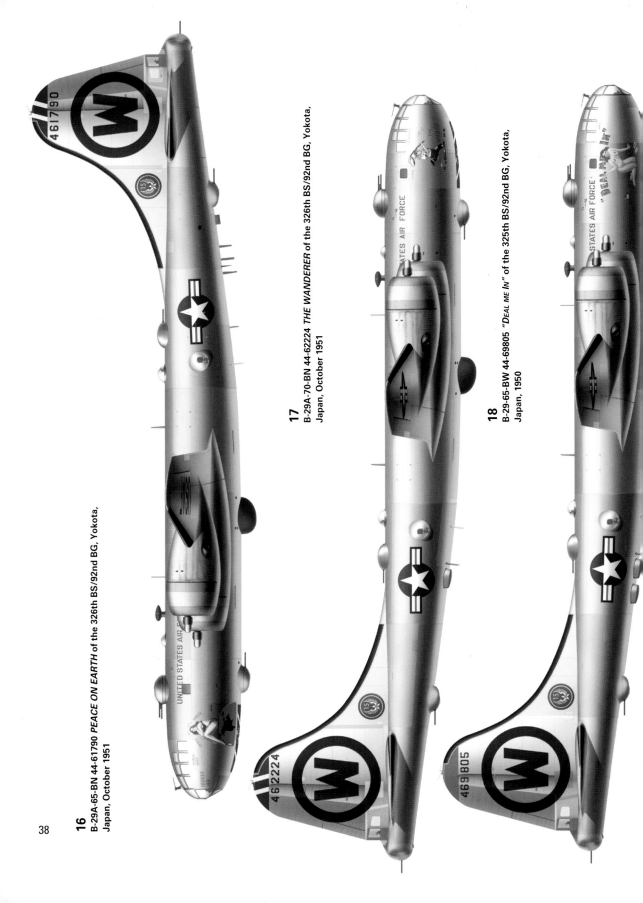

16
B-29A-65-BN 44-61790 *PEACE ON EARTH* of the 326th BS/92nd BG, Yokota, Japan, October 1951

17
B-29A-70-BN 44-62224 *THE WANDERER* of the 326th BS/92nd BG, Yokota, Japan, October 1951

18
B-29-65-BW 44-69805 *"DEAL ME IN"* of the 325th BS/92nd BG, Yokota, Japan, 1950

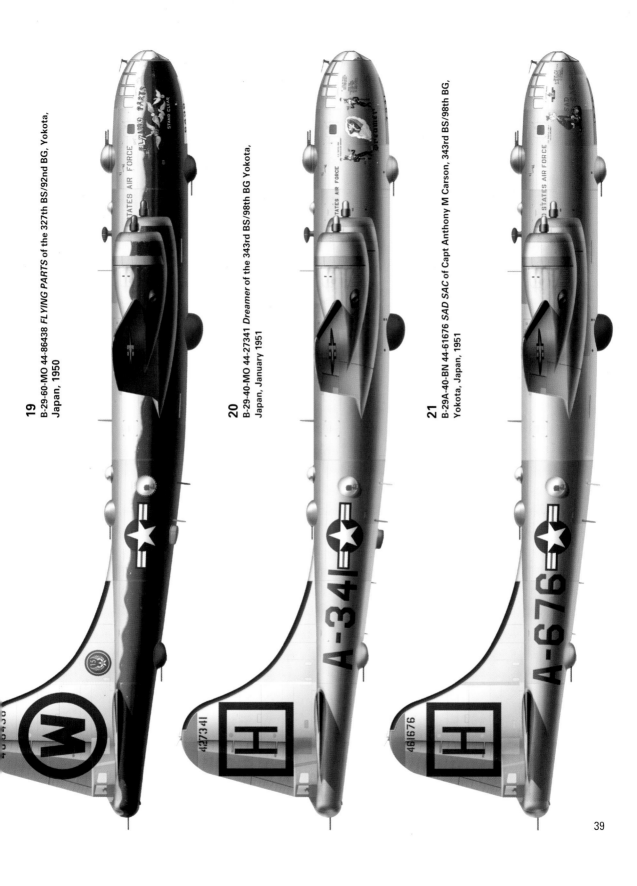

19
B-29-60-MO 44-86438 *FLYING PARTS* of the 327th BS/92nd BG, Yokota, Japan, 1950

20
B-29-40-MO 44-27341 *Dreamer* of the 343rd BS/98th BG Yokota, Japan, January 1951

21
B-29A-40-BN 44-61676 *SAD SAC* of Capt Anthony M Carson, 343rd BS/98th BG, Yokota, Japan, 1951

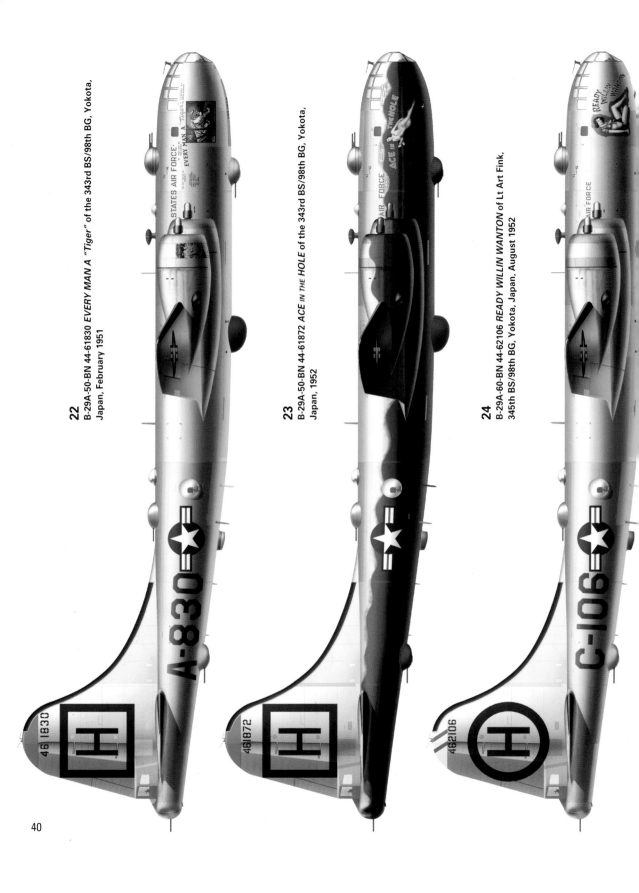

22
B-29A-50-BN 44-61830 *EVERY MAN A "Tiger"* of the 343rd BS/98th BG, Yokota,
Japan, February 1951

23
B-29A-50-BN 44-61872 *ACE IN THE HOLE* of the 343rd BS/98th BG, Yokota,
Japan, 1952

24
B-29A-60-BN 44-62106 *READY WILLIN WANTON* of Lt Art Fink,
345th BS/98th BG, Yokota, Japan, August 1952

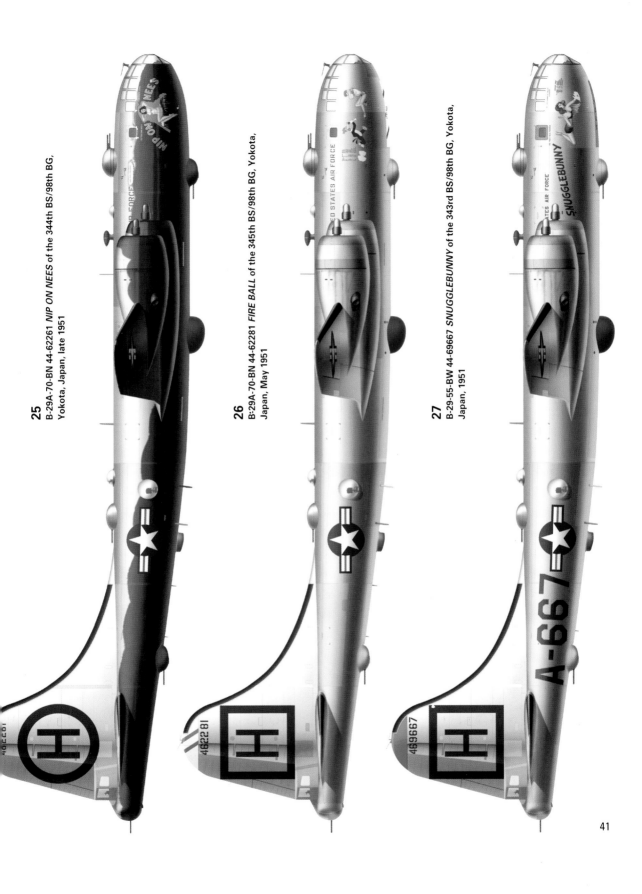

25
B-29A-70-BN 44-62261 *NIP ON NEES* of the 344th BS/98th BG,
Yokota, Japan, late 1951

26
B-29A-70-BN 44-62281 *FIRE BALL* of the 345th BS/98th BG, Yokota,
Japan, May 1951

27
B-29-55-BW 44-69667 *SNUGGLEBUNNY* of the 343rd BS/98th BG, Yokota,
Japan, 1951

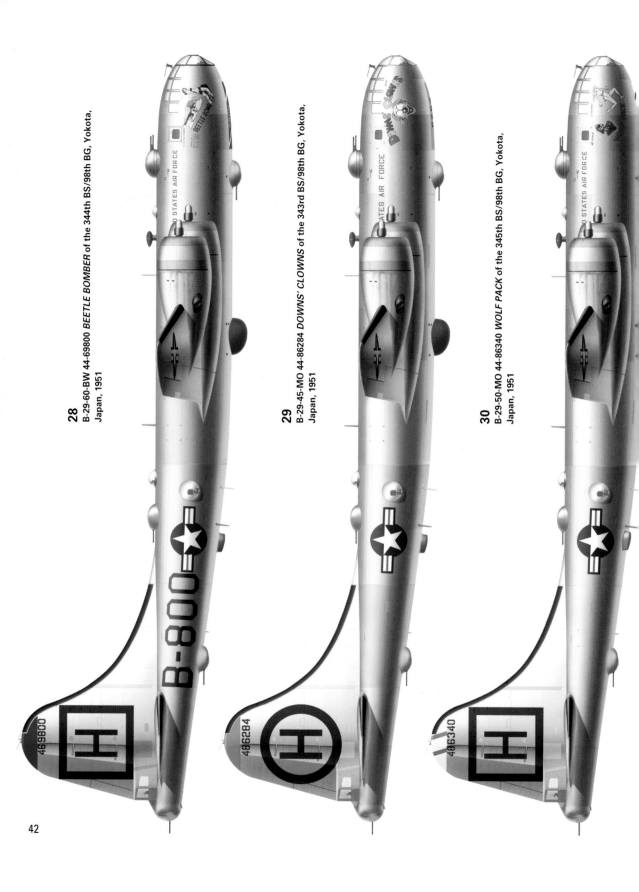

28
B-29-60-BW 44-69800 *BEETLE BOMBER* of the 344th BS/98th BG, Yokota, Japan, 1951

29
B-29-45-MO 44-86284 *DOWNS' CLOWNS* of the 343rd BS/98th BG, Yokota, Japan, 1951

30
B-29-50-MO 44-86340 *WOLF PACK* of the 345th BS/98th BG, Yokota, Japan, 1951

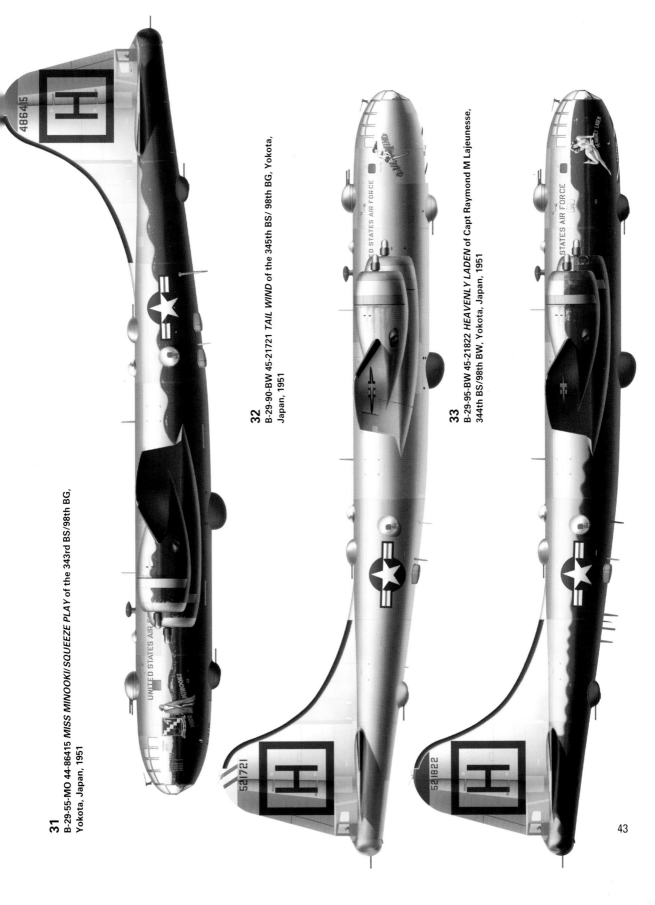

31
B-29-55-MO 44-86415 *MISS MINOOKI/SQUEEZE PLAY* of the 343rd BS/98th BG,
Yokota, Japan, 1951

32
B-29-90-BW 45-21721 *TAIL WIND* of the 345th BS/ 98th BG, Yokota,
Japan, 1951

33
B-29-95-BW 45-21822 *HEAVENLY LADEN* of Capt Raymond M Lajeunesse,
344th BS/98th BW, Yokota, Japan, 1951

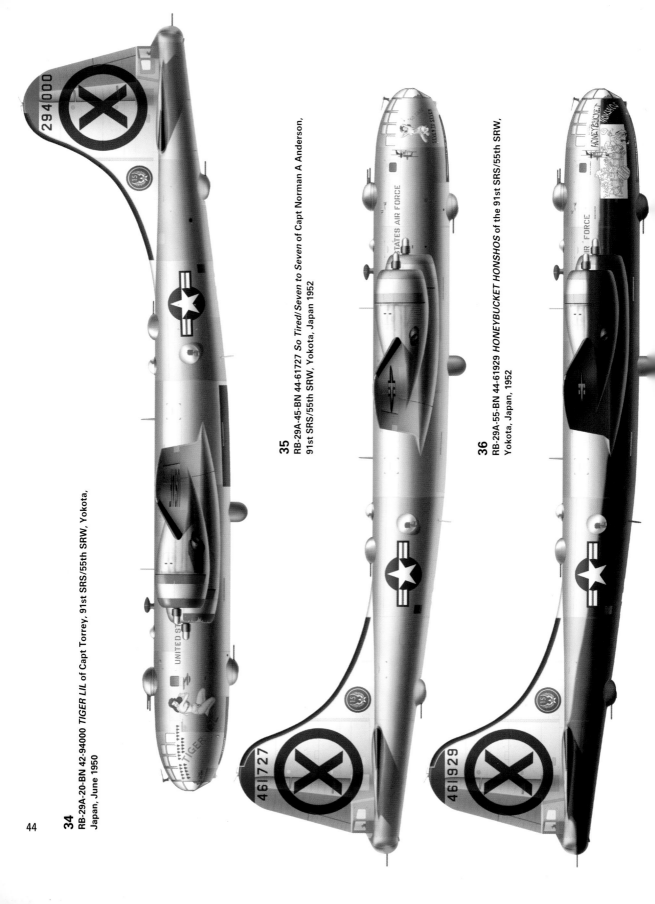

34
RB-29A-20-BN 42-94000 *TIGER LIL* of Capt Torrey, 91st SRS/55th SRW, Yokota, Japan, June 1950

35
RB-29A-45-BN 44-61727 *So Tired/Seven to Seven* of Capt Norman A Anderson, 91st SRS/55th SRW, Yokota, Japan 1952

36
RB-29A-55-BN 44-61929 *HONEYBUCKET HONSHOS* of the 91st SRS/55th SRW, Yokota, Japan, 1952

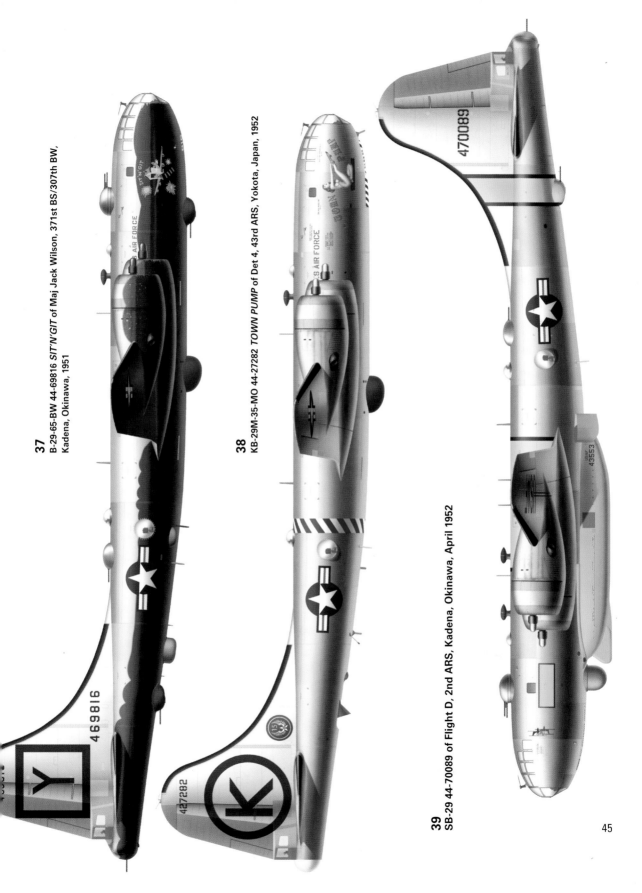

37
B-29-65-BW 44-69816 *SIT'N'GIT* of Maj Jack Wilson, 371st BS/307th BW,
Kadena, Okinawa, 1951

38
KB-29M-35-MO 44-27282 *TOWN PUMP* of Det 4, 43rd ARS, Yokota, Japan, 1952

39
SB-29 44-70089 of Flight D, 2nd ARS, Kadena, Okinawa, April 1952

This nose art section has been specially created by profile artist Mark Styling so as to better illustrate the colourful artworks worn by the Superfortresses featured in profile within this volume. These drawings have been produced following exhaustive cross-referencing with published bomb group histories, correspondence with surviving veterans and their families and the detailed study of original photographs.

An unidentified B-29 gunner loads a belt of 0.50-cal ammunition into the magazine of his top turret. Note the mount's cover resting on the fuselage behind him (*Roland T Speckman*)

Three minutes out from the target, eight B-29s of the 19th BG came under attack from 30+ MiG-15s. They managed to break through the escorts and immediately downed a bomber, which caught fire and crashed near the target. Gunfire from the MiGs damaged six more B-29s.

Navigator 1Lt Ralph Livengood of the 30th BS/19th BG recalled that his bomb group had 12 Superfortresses from three squadrons in the air. 'Six of our aeroplanes managed to get back to Okinawa', said Livengood. 'One diverted to Itazuke with wounded after battle damage was repaired. The pilot and bombardier were killed in another aeroplane as a result of air-to-air action by MiGs, forcing the co-pilot to fly back to Taegu and crash-land – it never flew again. A third B-29 ditched in the Yellow Sea with no survivors. A MiG shot yet another down over land, and no 'chutes were seen. A fifth bomber crash-landed in Seoul.

'Our tail gunner, S/Sgt Lyle Patterson, was credited with shooting down a MiG, and our crew had another damaged and a third as a probable. When we got back to Okinawa and were examining our aircraft for damage, we had three rounds left in our guns. We had fired everything else.'

After that horrendous mission – a precursor to one that would be called 'Black Tuesday' later in the year – Livengood remembered that, 'The strategy changed a bit. We would take off early at night or late in the day so we hit targets at first light or at dusk'.

The 12 April mission was not over when the 19th BG pulled off the target. A formation from the 307th BG, approaching the target independently rather than combining its defences with the other bomb groups, came under attack by the MiGs. One bomber was shot down and another badly damaged, forcing its crew to divert to K-13 Suwon airfield in South Korea. Ironically, although they were last over the target, the crews of the 98th BG escaped MiG attack. The escorting Thunderjets were credited with three probable MiG kills, but it was little compensation. Their job of flying fighter cover had not been quite so successful this time. Gen George E Stratemeyer, FEAF commander, candidly told Gen LeMay that the Thunderjets borrowed from SAC were too slow to cope with the MiGs, and that whenever possible the escort job would be performed by F-86s.

Even though he had urged their use in Korea, LeMay had never liked fighters. Differences with other generals over the usefulness of his F-84-equipped 27th FEW contributed to his later decision to get rid of SAC's fighter force altogether.

BRIDGE BUSTING

Questions about the success of the bridge-busting campaign have never been fully resolved. An April 1951 FEAF report made it seem that the B-29 force was performing very well. According to the report, the Superfortresses rendered 48 out of 60 bridges unserviceable, and also put 27 of 39 assigned marshalling yards out of action. But in the month leading up to the middle of April, FEAF Bomber Command lost a total of eight B-29s to combat and operational causes.

April 1951 also saw Gen Matthew B Ridgway relieve MacArthur as UN commander in Korea. The latter's differences with President Truman were many, but they included the general's desire to bomb his Chinese attackers on their own territory, perhaps with nuclear weapons if necessary. That job probably would not have been assigned to the B-29 units in the combat zone, for they had no training in nuclear delivery.

Ridgway was fully prepared to stay within the limits prescribed for him by Truman and by US policy, but with the approval of his bosses he set forth to inflict as many casualties on the enemy as possible. He approved the use of B-29s against troop concentrations, including one strike that was credited with killing some 600 soldiers.

In April 1951 the Chinese Peoples Volunteers were still on the offensive. Fifth Air Force boss Gen Partridge feared the Allies were in danger of being pushed into the sea, just as they had been the previous July. One concern was that the Chinese (the Americans did not yet know it was actually the Soviets they were fighting) might move MiGs into North Korea. Stratemeyer ordered Briggs to be ready to use his B-29s to support Fifth Air Force in attacking North Korean airfields.

Throughout much of April, working around periods when the weather was simply impossible, Superfortresses attacked airfields north of the 38th Parallel. While the B-29s worked over these priority targets by daylight, B-26 Invaders revisited them at night to hamper reconstruction efforts. MiG activity was moderate, but FEAF intelligence analysts noticed that the North Koreans still had about three dozen Il-10s, La-5s and Yak-9s. Soon, the foe would also field a significant number of Polikarpov Po-2 biplanes, these aircraft inflicting serious damage during daring night raids on Allied bases.

The campaign against the airfields continued into May 1951. In retrospect, it now appears that the communists may never have intended to move MiGs south of the Yalu, but Allied leaders had no way of knowing this. Historian Robert F Futrell credited the enemy's air force with 'general lethargy' during May 1951. It may have been a time when the Soviets were rotating fighter regiments. Within weeks, an FEAF intelligence report asserted that, 'more proficient (MiG) pilots have arrived'.

An after-dark strike by eight B-29s on 21 May was directed against Chinese troops massing on highways near Hangye and Chunchon, in central South Korea. The radar-directed bomb drop amounted to a close air support mission within eyesight of friendly troops, and was credited by the ground commander on the scene as being 'utterly amazing'.

A combined night attack by B-29s and B-26s on 7 June showered air-bursting 500-lb bombs on advancing Chinese troops, also in central South Korea. The Superfortresses returned to attack these troop concentrations on two further, successive nights.

Three days later, in a ceremony held at Haneda airport in Tokyo, Gen O P Weyland replaced Lt Gen George E Stratemeyer, who had suffered a heart attack the previous month, as commander of FEAF. At about the same time, Maj Gen Frank F Everest replaced Gen Partridge as commander of Fifth Air Force, which had the job of providing fighter support to B-29 formations.

The seasons run the full range in Korea, and the heat of summer provided no relief. On 9 July, aggressive MiG pilots intercepted six 19th BG Superfortresses as the bombers pulled off their target – the ubiquitous airfield at Sinuiju. Escorting F-86 pilots shot down a MiG, and a B-29 gunner was credited with another, but the behaviour of the enemy pilots was a sign that things were not getting better.

RECCE 'SUPERFORTS'

In August the 91st SRS acquired a unit called Detachment 3, made up of three RB-50G Superfortress electronic reconnaissance aircraft sent to the FEAF on temporary duty (TDY) by SAC, Each aircraft carried a crew of 16, and had two sealed bomb-bays and six stations for 'Ravens', later commonly called electronic warfare officers. The RB-50Gs were crammed with electronic intelligence equipment.

The first RB-50G to see combat, with a crew headed by Capt James L Ford, took off from Yokota on 12 August for a 7-hour 15-minute mission monitoring hostile electronic emissions. Ford's aircraft was 47-133, named *Ramey's Ramblers* after the US air base in Puerto Rico. Another of the aircraft was RB-50G Superfortress 47-151 *Caribbean Queen*, piloted by Major Zane Hall, which was marked with silhouettes of crows to indicate its successful electronics intelligence missions.

The three RB-50Gs eventually flew missions in Korea in the summer and autumn of 1951, before returning to their stateside assignments. An Air Force commendation letter credits Ford and his crew with 16 combat missions and 201 combat flying hours (plus an 'aggressive spirit and the will to see the job done') before the RB-50Gs were withdrawn.

On 25 August, Col Harris E Rogner, vice commander of FEAF Bomber Command, led 35 Superfortresses of the 19th, 98th and 307th BGs against the North Korean city of Rashin, which had previously been off limits because of its proximity to the Soviet Union. The bombers received a partial escort from F2H-2 Banshees and F9F Panthers from the aircraft carrier USS *Essex* (CV-9). 'We clobbered them', Rogner later said.

Three RB-50G Superfortresses began flying reconnaissance missions in Korea on 12 August 1951, and remained in-theatre until 1 November that same year. Like 47-122 seen here, the three combat RB-50Gs were delivered from the factory as B-50Bs and converted to RB-50G standard (as shown), with internal changes not visible when viewing the aircraft from the outside (*US Air Force*)

One of the bomber pilots that day was a young lieutenant, E J 'Mac' McGill, who in later years became manager of the premier B-29 website, as well as a mystery writer.

McGill had joined the 28th BS/ 19th BG at Kadena earlier that same month, and immediately began daylight bombing targets in North Korea. 'Some of the men wondered, with reason, whether they would ever see home again', McGill said in an interview. 'Each day, MiG-15s swarmed aloft from Chinese airfields north of the Yalu, sliced through the thin screen of F-86s

44-61951 was an RB-29A of the 91st SRS, its nose boasting an Irish/Scottish-looking pin-up and the barely visible name *OUR L'LASS*. The flash of paint on the nose wheel door was typical of the period (*Mike Moffitt*)

south of the river and plunged into the bombers. "Take any aeroplane you want", my uncle told me while in flight school, "but don't take B-29s"'.

McGill's first mission, on 25 August, was one of the longest of the war – the 11-hour strike on the Rashin railway yards up near the Soviet border. 'This was really stretching it. The crew was scared. They were silent the whole time. The flak looked like a Disney time-frame photo of a flower blooming. All of a sudden, I grew up'.

McGill's aeroplane was hit, but no MiGs appeared. Days later, however, over North Korea, McGill peered from his co-pilot's seat to see a lone enemy fighter coming after him and his wingmen.

'This MiG went right through our formation. Then, the SOB stalled out. His nose pointed up. Everybody fired at him. Our top gun opened up. Our bombardier was on to him, blazing away. Nobody got him. The MiG lost altitude, recovered, and flew away. When we got home, almost every B-29 had had bullet holes put into it by other B-29s!'

McGill had started out as an enlisted weatherman in the newly-independent USAF of 1948-49. He entered flight training with Class 50-G, learning to fly in T-6s and TB-25s, and graduating on 16 December 1950. His first flight in a B-29 was at Randolph AFB, Texas, on 22 January 1951 with the 3510th Primary Training Wing (Basic), which 'had been cranked up quickly because of the North Korean invasion'.

When he joined the 321st BS for combat crew training at Forbes AFB, Kansas, and began flying on 12 June, no B-29s were available, so new pilots flew in C-47s – 'No wonder we were so dangerous'. Within weeks, McGill was dodging flak and MiGs. 'We faced discomfort, difficulty, long hours of boredom punctuated by moments of sheer terror, and statistics which seemed to say that we had no chance of survival'.

Even without the enemy, crews were uneasy about flying the B-29. One crewman described the bomber as 'loud, shaky and vulnerable', whilst another said it 'was too old for the war in Korea'. Never effective at high altitude, the B-29 was prevented by enemy flak from attacking at lower levels. 'We flew at a terrible altitude' says McGill. '20,000 to 25,000 ft. We couldn't fly higher with a heavy bombload'.

Brig Gen Joe W Kelly became commander of FEAF Bomber Command on 30 September, replacing Gen Briggs. It was the high point of a calm

In August 1951, 1Lt (later Maj) E J 'Mac' McGill joined the 28th BS/ 19th BG at Kadena Air Base as a B-29 Superfortress co-pilot. He is better known as a mystery novel writer thanks to publication of his crime novel *Immaculate in Black* in 1991. McGill survived a B-29 crash that destroyed an aircraft, as well as MiGs and anti-aircraft fire (*E J McGill*)

Air Training Command continued to turn out not only pilots but navigators, radio operators and gunners during the Korean War, which meant that even B-29s used in training were likely to be fully armed. This view of a home front Superfortress shows a TB-29 of Air Training Command flying over Randolph Air Force Base, Texas, with a crew under training in preparation for a posting to FEAF, and action over Korea. Boeing's Wichita, Kansas, facility was the builder of aircraft 44-70064 (*US Air Force*)

While B-29 crews fought in Korea, training of new crews was ramped up at stateside bases. These Superfortresses belong to the 3510th Combat Crew Training Wing, which supplied FEAF with replacement crews (*via Norman Taylor*)

period of some weeks when the MiGs seemed to be leaving the B-29s alone. But now Kelly was tasked to attack airfields around Chongchon, in North Korea, which were close enough to the Yalu for the MiGs to be expected to mount a defence.

At this juncture, the Superfortresses were averaging 16 combat sorties a day, including at least one aircraft used to distribute psychological warfare leaflets (this job was called 'the paper route') and another carrying out a SHORAN-directed attack on marshalling yards at night.

The 98th BG was the first to be equipped with SHORAN, followed by the 19th and 307th. The system combined the work of two AN/APN-2 radar beacon ground stations of the USAF's 1st SHORAN Beacon Flight with the AN/APN-3 transceiver carried aboard a B-29. The system was more commonly used with the B-26, which operated at night from June 1950, but eventually each bomb group had two or three AN/APN-3-equipped Superfortresses, which acted as pathfinders in poor weather.

SHORAN reduced the circular error probability (CEP) of a bomb drop from 2000 ft to 485 ft, but it required a focused crew, superb navigation and good geographic and climatic data. The 13 October attack on a North Korean airfield complex by the 307th BG made use of SHORAN bombing, but the results were mixed at best – it was estimated that only 24 of the 278 bombs dropped hit the runway, which was speedily rebuilt.

As previously mentioned, we know today that the Soviets never intended to move MiG-15s across the river into North Korea, but in the autumn of 1951 no subject worried Allied military leaders more than the possibility of enemy air bases located within easy flying distance of the frontlines. Kelly reluctantly decided that if airfields in North Korea were

to be neutralised, the Superfortresses would have to make formation day attacks, using SHORAN to guide the entire force. The time of day for such raids would be determined by the availability of F-86s to fly high cover. Since only four SHORAN approaches to any given target were available, and North Korea was in any event a confined sector of airspace, enemy anti-aircraft gunners would have plenty of opportunity to make life miserable for Superfortress crews.

OUTLAW OUT

Five days prior to the unsuccessful SHORAN mission of 13 October, the crew of Kadena-based B-29-MO 42-65306 *The Outlaw* (named after the Howard Hughes movie starring Jane Russell) of the 28th BS/19th BG had experienced an abruptly curtailed sortie. Co-pilot 'Mac' McGill had settled into his right-hand front seat for a planned mission, thinking that everything would be just fine that day. After all, *The Outlaw* had survived the very first combat mission of the Korean War and, more recently, had been hit by cannon fire from a MiG-15 and been repaired.

McGill's crew was taxiing out behind an SB-17G search and rescue aircraft when it ground-looped, ploughed into a ditch and damaged the tip of its right wing. It is unclear whether the mishap to the SB-17 had any direct influence on what happened next to *The Outlaw.*

Cleared for take-off, with aircraft commander Don Thompson handling the controls, McGill's B-29 shot forward and accelerated to 70 knots. On the intercom, the engineer's voice boomed, 'I've got problems with number one', referring to the engine. Another crewmember then announced, 'We've got a fire'.

Thompson elected to continue the take-off run, although only 5000 ft of runway remained. Clamouring and burning, the B-29 gained some 'lift'. For an instant, it seemed the bomber might leap into the air, giving the crew merciful time to cope with the emergency. McGill remembers a brief moment when he felt sure everything would be okay, followed by a long and awful moment when he knew it wouldn't.

The Outlaw crashed, and McGill was heaved forward against his seat straps. On the intercom, somebody cried out. There was a heavy thumping sound, followed by a staccato of noise as the aircraft broke apart. Fuel gushed from a ruptured tank. McGill unstrapped, emerged from a gaping open space in the nose of the aircraft and saw Thompson climbing out, drenched in fuel. Every crewmember of *The Outlaw* survived unhurt, and went on to continue flying risky missions over North Korea.

On 18 October nine B-29s of the 19th BG went after Saamcham airfield and nine more from the 98th BG attacked Taechon. The 19th BG Superfortresses dumped 306 100-lb bombs on the Saamcham runway, but the 98th bombers missed a rendezvous point with their fighter cover and ended up going to a secondary target.

There was a horrific loss when one of the 98th BG B-29s returned to Yokota. Piloted by a Lt Mason, the Superfortress's crew was completing their first mission together, and there were also extra personnel on board. Struggling to land, the B-29 attempted a go-around with its bomb-bay doors open for reasons that remain unclear. It never made it, crashing instead into the bowling alley at Yokota, where it erupted in flames. Eight men perished and six survived.

The remains of Martin-built B-29-MO Superfortress 42-65306 *The Outlaw* (named after the Howard Hughes movie starring Jane Russell) of the 28th BS/19th BG are seen at Kadena shortly after the aircraft crashed on take-off on 8 October 1951. *The Outlaw* had been one of four bombers that flew the first Superfortress combat mission on 27 (according to one account) or 28 June 1950 (*E J McGill*)

When another 98th BG mission on 21 October also ran afoul because the bombers failed to link up with the fighters, Sabre pilot 1Lt Martin Bambrick wrote in his journal that 'Gabreski was blind!' As Bambrick saw it, the great World War 2 ace Col Francis S Gabreski was responsible for the failure of Sabres and Superfortresses to link up. Fighter escort worked better the next day, when nine 19th BG B-29s managed to rendezvous with 24 F-84s on a mission that finally brought bombs raining down successfully on Taechon airfield.

Almost as soon as the bombs fell, 40 MiG-15s drew the F-84s away from the bombers. While fighter-versus-fighter combat took place several miles from the B-29s, a trio of MiG-15s swooped down and attacked the bombers so rapidly that gunners had no opportunity to shoot back. One B-29 suffered flak hits and then came under fire from a MiG. The ambush appeared not to have been planned, but the B-29 was a goner. The pilot nursed it to the coast, where the crew baled out and was rescued.

The mission on 23 October, dubbed 'Black Tuesday', lives in the memory of B-29 crews as their darkest day of the Korean War. Eight B-29s from the 307th BG (of nine that began the mission) went forth to bomb Namsi airfield at Sinuiju, along the Yalu. The weather was supposed to be clear and, sadly, it was. The day began when Sabres downed two MiGs near the Yalu, but subsequently withdrew before an escort of Thunderjets proved unable to protect their bomber charges.

MiGs caught the B-29s over their target, the size of the communist fighter force having been variously estimated at somewhere between 55 (Futrell) and 150 (research by B-29 veteran E J McGill). Three B-29s were shot down, and all but one of the surviving bombers received major damage. A number of these were carrying dead and wounded crewmen aboard when they made emergency landings in Japan and Korea. Only one B-29 (44-87760) returned safely to its base. The F-84s scored one MiG kill, which was credited to Navy exchange pilot Lt (later Capt) Walter Schirra, who subsequently became a Mercury and Apollo astronaut, but the Thunderjets also lost one of their own.

The first trio of Superfortresses over the target was 'A' Flight of the 371st BS/307th BG, consisting of B-29s piloted by Capt Clarence I Fogler (44-61816), Capt James R Lewis (44-87750) and Capt Robert M Krumm (44-94045). Krumm's aircraft was among those shot down in the first minutes of the battle. The second trio of Superfortresses consisted of 'B' Flight of the 372nd BS/307th BG, comprising B-29s piloted by Capt James A Foulks Jr (44-71940), 1Lt William Fleeter

(44-27347) and a third pilot whose name is not on record (44-86295). Foulks, too, was shot down in the first minutes of the MiG attack. The third, and final, brace of B-29s on the Namsi raid – 'C' Flight – was a formation of two B-29s (or three, according to the McGill account, which puts nine bombers on the raid rather than eight). The names of the other pilot, or pilots, are not on record, but the number one aircraft in the formation was flown

by Capt Thomas L Shields of the 370th BS/307th BG. In his account for the US government, historian Futrell recounted Shields' fate;

'Between their initial point and the target, all of the ships in "Charlie" Flight were under attack, and as the bombers dropped their loads and broke left, some confusion on the part of escorting Thunderjets left them inadequately protected. Actually, however, the Thunderjets were so badly outclassed that they could not offer too much protection. Most of the attacking MiGs flew normal pursuit curves, but some of them dived downward through the bomber formation so as to deny the Thunderjet pilots or the Superfortress gunners much opportunity to fire. One flight of MiGs came straight up under the B-29s with all guns blazing. Capt Shields coaxed his B-29 back to the coast, where his crew baled out, but Shields did not get free from the stricken ship in time to save his own life.'

McGill, who was a B-29 co-pilot in Korea but was not on the Namsi strike, summed up the results of 'Black Tuesday' as follows;

'Three B-29s were shot down "within a matter of minutes". Three heavily damaged B-29s landed at Kimpo. Two badly damaged B-29s (44-27347 and 44-86295) were transferred to the depot for disposition. Of the three B-29s that eventually made it back to Kadena, two were badly shot up. Thirty-four crewmembers were declared missing in action. The *Pacific Stars and Stripes*, the newspaper for servicemen in the Far East, ran the headline the next day ''superforts' Tangle With MiGs In Toughest Week of Air War'.'

McGill remembers the mood aboard his B-29, readying for another mission, just after the 'Black Tuesday' disaster. 'It was like a funeral', he said. 'There was silence over the intercom. "Start engines", the pilot ordered. Again, silence. "Cleared to taxi out". Again, silence. There was none of the usual chatter that preceded a take-off. As the B-29 trundled down the taxiway, a radio call came in. "Taxi back to the hardstand and shut down". US Air Force chief of staff Hoyt S Vandenberg had personally ordered a halt to daylight bomber operations over North Korea'.

Prior to this directive being issued, however, the bloody results of the Namsi raid had not prevented Kelly from sending eight 98th BG Superfortresses to attack a railway bridge at Sunchon, just south of 'MiG Alley', 24 hours after 'Black Tuesday'. Morale cannot have been high aboard the bombers as they headed north, Escorted by Meteor F 8 fighters of the Royal Australian Air Force's No 77 Sqn, as well as F-84 Thunderjets, the Superfortresses nevertheless ran into an aggressive ambush by MiGs.

Long before 'Black Tuesday' (23 October 1951), some B-29s wore black undersides to shield them from enemy searchlights – these machines were photographed several months prior to this date. After the 23rd, however, black garb became routine, and occasionally cloaked the entire aircraft, not just the underside. The lead bomber in this shot is 44-84110, built by Bell in Atlanta (*Gene Deatrick*)

B-29 gunners were credited with a MiG-15 destroyed, but the Soviet jets pressed their attacks home and shot down a bomber over Wonsan harbour.

Three days later, again with Meteor and Thunderjet escorts, Superfortresses returned to the bridge at Sinuiju. The approach to the target was made over the Yellow Sea in the belief (correct, as it turned out) that MiG pilots would not fight over water, since their air force had no apparatus to rescue a pilot downed at sea. The Superfortresses encountered MiGs only after making landfall, but the fighting was furious. One bomber gunner was credited with a MiG and a B-29 was severely damaged.

28 October was the final day of sustained daytime B-29 operations in the face of the MiG threat, the 98th BG sending eight Superfortresses to strike a bridge at Sunchon. MiGs were seen in the area but they did not engage the bombers. During the month of October, FEAF had lost seven F-86s, five Superfortresses, two Thunderjets and an RF-80 in battle. The five B-29s almost equalled the previous figure of six lost in the entire war. Alarmed at these losses, Gen Vandenberg made a quick trip to the region, where he received discouraging reports from B-29 crewmembers.

'Mac' McGill remembers the general's visit well, the pilot stepping down from his bomber after an uneventful mission to learn that Vandenberg had just flown in from the Pentagon.

Staff officers swarmed around the chief of staff, anxious to hand him briefing papers. A colonel wanted to hand him a memorandum to study. 'Get rid of that stuff', Vandenberg snapped. 'I want to talk to a tail gunner. I want B-29 crewmembers around me here. I don't want to talk to anyone else'. According to McGill, bomber crews told Vandenberg that their 0.50-cal machine guns were just about useless. The general asked a member of McGill's crew about the armament. 'It's worthless', the man replied. 'Anything would be better than what we've got'. An Air Force sergeant pointed out that several of the men were officially credited with shooting down MiGs, but none seriously believed they had really done so. Today, the best evidence is that they were right.

When Vandenberg returned to Washington DC, he was considering the prospect that the United States might have to withdraw its B-29s from the Korean theatre entirely. Curiously enough, however, there is no evidence that anyone suggested replacing the B-29s with newer B-50s. It remains unclear, even today, why the B-50 – which flew reconnaissance missions in the combat zone – was never used as a bomber in the Korean War. In the end, the only decision made was one to strengthen the F-86 force, but the enemy was increasing its fighter arsenal, too.

By the end of 1951, a handful of MiGs had been moved to the North Korean side of the Yalu, and the MiG-15bis model, with its improved engine, was being introduced to the combat zone. For a brief period, it appeared that the Soviets – whom the Americans steadfastly believed were Chinese – intended to extend their airpower to the battle lines and beyond. On at least one occasion, MiGs ventured south of Seoul, which was now in UN hands. Weyland reported to his superiors that there was a 'serious danger' of the enemy challenging US air superiority. Briefly, Tupolev Tu-2 bombers were also seen, and engaged, along the Yalu.

The MiG threat to the B-29 force was one reason why Vandenberg and the Pentagon brass reversed their long-standing policy and agreed to move a second fighter wing of F-86s to Korea. By the end of 1951, the 51st FIW had joined the 4th in patrolling 'MiG Alley'.

At a critical meeting on 28 October, FEAF Bomber Command boss Kelly announced that henceforth B-29s would operate only at night. He also proposed to significantly expand the use of SHORAN to improve their bombing accuracy.

While a crash programme was launched to install SHORAN on more B-29s, FEAF Bomber Command began a series of airfield raids on 4 November. As the month progressed, and more SHORAN-equipped Superfortresses became available, the size of the raids increased. Most crews had no SHORAN experience, and there were teething troubles, but as year-end approached, operations against the airfields began to produce good damage estimates.

On the night of 8 November, ground-based anti-aircraft fire connected with a B-29 flying a propaganda leaflet mission. The aircraft was Renton-built B-29A-20-BN Superfortress 42-93974 of the 343rd BS/98th BG, based at Yokota. After being hit by flak near Chongju, the damaged bomber was coaxed by pilot Capt Donald G Bigham (the only member of the crew who belonged to the 342nd BS/98th BG) back towards the island of Paengnyong-do – better known as K-53 or 'P-Y-do' to Americans. Located just west of the 38th Parallel off the coast of North Korea, it was held (as it is today) by friendly troops. The island is about seven miles from the mainland.

Of the dozen men on board, all except Bigham were rescued, one by a helicopter and the others by American and South Korean infantry patrols on 'P-Y-do'. Several were wounded when the Superfortress was hit or during the bale-out itself. Bigham became a PoW, which suggests that his parachute drifted east across seven miles of water to the mainland – or, he baled out first.

On 4 December, a B-29 was caught in the glare of a very potent enemy weapon – the radar-controlled searchlight – and MiGs moved in to inflict serious damage. A second such incident happened on 23 December. Soon afterward, Invaders began working with the B-29s in a coordinated effort to carry out night attacks against the searchlights.

Namsi airfield, the target on the infamous 'Bloody Tuesday' raid, should have been a word to inspire dread on the part of Superfortress crewmembers. Similarly, worries about MiGs and flak should have prompted morale problems. S/Sgt Jesse Richey, a flight engineer with the 345th BS/98th BG at Yokota, remembered that neither was the case. When Namsi airfield came up in the briefing as the target for a night mission on 5 December, 'the name did not mean anything to us. Moreover, I can't say that our morale was poor. I had lost three good friends from flight engineer school on the "Black Tuesday" raid, but I felt I would be all right. We were going to be flying at night this time, and we believed we would have little problem with MiGs or flak. We were half right.'

As flight engineer, Richey sat in a rearward-facing seat immediately behind the co-pilot of Renton-built B-29A-70-BN 44-62281 *Fireball*, a veteran bomber with a likeness of *Woody Woodpecker* on the nose;

'We had solid flak for 12 to 14 minutes going in to the target. I had curtains over my window to prevent light from escaping, so I couldn't see the anti-aircraft fire, but I could hear it – a kind of a crinkling sound. As it intensified, it sounded like a hailstorm. Our aircraft was punctured by quite a few holes, although none was very large.'

Busily monitoring engine instruments, Richey had no way to observe the bombers' arrival over the target, but other veterans say the 98th BG retained good formation discipline. At least, as Richey had expected, there was no sign of MiGs. 'As soon as we delivered the bombs, our pilot made a diving turn and got the hell out of there'.

Richey eventually flew 37 missions, including eight daylight operations, without suffering a scratch. Still, as 1951 drew to a close, Superfortress crews knew they were confronting an enemy who would do everything in his power to defend himself.

A SOLDIER'S VIEW

Nothing captured the imagination of B-29 crews more than the news that they would be going to a target in North Korea that was heavily defended by searchlights, anti-aircraft guns and MiGs. But to foot soldiers with their boots on the ground, those daylight missions to the frontlines were of critical importance. One American soldier who remembers the B-29 is John T Jones. He served as a sergeant in the US Army's 17th Regimental Combat Team, and in later years he became author of the Taylor Jones detective and western novels. Jones never knew that a pilot of one of those B-29s, E J McGill, also became a mystery writer in later years.

'When I was serving as a forward observer for the 81 mm mortars on Hill 1243 in December 1951', remembered Jones, 'my radioman and I were lifted into the air in our sleeping bags in the middle of a pitch-black winter night by a thunderous ground shaking. We were not far from the summit, called the "Punch Bowl", which had been the scene of bitter fighting. A B-29 flew in over the "Punch Bowl" and dropped 500-lb bombs on the mountain across from us, about 1300 yards peak-to-peak. They also dropped cluster bombs, which we called "Butterfly Bombs".

'The bombing was made by radar. Friendly troops on our hill were under the heaviest artillery bombardment of the Korean War, according to the *Stars and Stripes* newspaper. The three air strikes we got every day from the Navy Corsairs and the Air Force Mustangs gave us a break from the Chinese fire, but did not solve our problem.

'We did have concerns about the B-29s because our own artillery had blasted us three times the second night we were on the line – they had the correct range, I think, but too low a trajectory to avoid clipping us on the top of our hill. As it turned out, the B-29s did an excellent job, giving us a lot of relief from the enemy.

'Anyway', concluded Jones, 'I felt for the poor Chinese soldiers that were catching those 500-lb bombs'.

From the start of the Korean War in June 1950 until 'Black Tuesday' in October 1951, B-29 Superfortress crews spent part of their time providing direct air support to ground combat troops like these soldiers of the US Army's 2nd Infantry Division. After 'Black Tuesday', when the MiG-15 all but drove the Superfortress out of the daylight sky for good, the B-29 was no longer a tool for the infantryman (*US Army*)

1952

By the start of 1952, the Korean peninsula was weary of war, the battle lines had largely stabilised in a way that reminded soldiers of another era of trench warfare earlier in the century, and the Superfortress campaign was being conducted at night. With black bottoms to accompany their often colourful nose art, the bombers went north into enemy territory mostly during nocturnal hours, although they occasionally supported frontline troops during the day.

UN commander-in-chief, Gen Matthew B Ridgway, viewed the B-29 as an important weapon in his arsenal. At Ridgway's request, FEAF Bomber Command carried out two colossal (63 aircraft participated in the first and 60 in the second) Superfortress raids on Pyongyang on 3 and 5 January, with the goal of burning the city to the ground with incendiary bombs. As Clay Blair wrote in *The Forgotten War*, Radio Pyongyang reported that 'the entire city burned like a furnace for two days', but analysis conducted after the attacks concluded that owing to the presence of fire-retarding snow on Pyongyang rooftops, barely 35 per cent of the city was actually destroyed.

As late as January 1952, the 91st SRS, now commanded by Lt Col Vincent M Crane, was still in the process of converting its RB-29 reconnaissance aircraft for night operations. It was not an easy process, for in order to be guided by SHORAN, and to be above much of the foe's anti-aircraft fire, the RB-29 needed to operate at ceilings greater than 20,000 ft. But the M-46 photoflash bomb used to illuminate targets did not provide enough light when dropped from that height. Later in the year the problem would be solved when the squadron received the more powerful M-120 photoflash bomb.

Other technical problems also stood in the way, some of which were resolved by using short focal-length

These B-29 target photos were described by a crewman as follows. 'These were taken on bombing missions over North Korea for the purpose of assessing the accuracy of the mission. They were shot at night by the automatic camera on the aeroplane, triggered by the light of photoflash bombs timed to go off as the other bombs hit the ground'. All these years later, we do not know which mission this was (*Richard Iler*)

night cameras with photoelectric shutters that were tripped by the light of flash bombs.

DARK WAR

The foe's night defences were a serious concern. When Superfortress crews were ordered once again to attack the formidably defended Sinuiju airfield along the Yalu, FEAF Bomber Command boss Brig Gen Joe W Kelly waited until the night of 26 January 1952, when a thick layer of low-slung cloud blocked the enemy's searchlights. Using the SHORAN navigation system that linked ground stations with the AN/APN-3 transceiver aboard suitably-equipped B-29s, the 98th BG set forth from Yokota and attacked the all-too-familiar airfield in an eventless mission.

Still, the number of radar-directed flak batteries and searchlights was increasing rapidly, as was the size of the MiG force operating at night.

26 January also marked the first occasion that B-29s operated jointly with B-26 Invaders in attacking a logistical choke point that connected Pyongyang and Wonsan – such collaboration would continue through to 11 March. These SHORAN raids were aimed at troops and equipment, rather than installations, and the results were, at best, questionable. They were intended to support Operation *Strangle*, which was a larger campaign aimed at Chinese forces by UN commander Gen Ridgway.

The Superfortress force continued to suffer about half of its aircraft losses due to non-combat causes. Many of these accidents occurred when pilots with less than optimum experience were at the controls. For example, on 7 February 1952 45-21721 *TAIL WIND* hit a 475-ft hill northeast of Yokota and killed everyone on board. The pilot, Col John Grabel, who was the 98th BG's operations officer, had relatively little B-29 time, and was apparently flying the aircraft when it crashed – not Maj Dan Smith, the instructor pilot, who was sat in the right seat.

With a suitably decorated signpost identifying the parking spot for Renton-built B-29 44-61874 of the 344th BS/98th BG, the veteran bomber basks in the sunshine at Yokota in its mostly-black paint scheme that was intended to foil North Korean searchlights (*Roland T Speckman*)

Some of the aerial bombing in support of Operation *Strangle* was carried out in coordination with tactical air strikes by Fifth Air Force F-80s, F-84s and B-26s, and as such was part of an effort dubbed Operation *Saturate*. In late March Superfortresses hit rail and supply targets in Pyongyang, Sinanju and Sinhung-ni in support of this campaign.

On 15 March Brig Gen Wiley D Ganey became head of FEAF Bomber Command, replacing Brig Gen Joe W Kelly. It was at this juncture that the Air Force combat wing replaced the combat group as the service's primary fighting formation. In this text, the term BW for Bombardment Wing (Medium) will replace BG for Bombardment Group (Medium) at this point.

Elsewhere in the USAF, the service inactivated combat group headquarters and made each combat wing directly responsible for the operation of its squadrons. Soon after Ganey came on the job, the HQ of the 98th and 307th BWs ceased reporting to SAC and became part of FEAF Bomber Command. Incredibly, SAC was then in the process of phasing out the B-29, despite it remaining the only bomber in its class available to men participating in an actual shooting war.

A crash landing at K-14 Kimpo Air Base, near Seoul, saved the crew of a Superfortress that sustained serious battle damage on 22 April, 44-61872 being a B-29A-50-BN of the 98th BG that was known at various times in its service career as *SAC's appeal* and *ACE IN THE HOLE*. It appears that all in the crew survived the impromptu arrival at Kimpo, but 44-61872 did not. For a period of time, there was a veritable junkyard of B-29 bits and pieces at Kimpo, not far from the main terminal building, which was itself still pocked with bullet holes from strafing by North Korean fighters in the first days of the war.

On 12 May Gen Mark W Clark replaced Gen Matthew B Ridgway as commander-in-chief of the UN Command and of US forces in Korea. Clark was aloof, but friends admired his competence and addressed him by his middle name, Wayne. He achieved numerous successes on the battlefield, yet one of his US Military Academy upper classmen, Gen Omar Bradley, branded him 'a lightweight, with an egotistic streak'. However, historians view West Pointer Clark as one of the most important American military leaders of the 20th century. He was to become bitter about the outcome of the Korean War, and to view himself as the only American general ever to conclude a conflict that did not end in victory.

KWAKSAN LOSSES

On 10 June the 19th BG sent four Superfortresses to bomb railway bridges at Kwaksan. The B-29 crews ran into furious air defences, 24 searchlights keeping them constantly illuminated while flak batteries stalked their prey. They were then attacked by about 12 jet fighters – apparently MiGs – which shot down two of the bombers and damaged a third badly enough that it had to land at Kimpo.

Having moved from day to night to elude the persistent MiG-15, the Superfortress crews now knew that the hours of darkness were no longer safe for them either. Morale slumped in the 19th BG, and Bomber Command boss Ganey reacted to the losses by questioning whether an electronic countermeasures capability could be added to the B-29. He also ordered that all B-29s not yet painted black on the undersides be

Despite their nocturnal finish these 28th BG Superfortresses were photographed bombing a target during a rare daylight raid in 1952. In the centre of the shot is Glenn L Martin-built B-29-MO 44-86375, a single bomb being visible dropping away from its forward bay (*John Kalogeris*)

Airman 2nd Class Marcus E Padilla sits at the left gunner's blister position, operating the remote control for his machine guns. He belonged to a crew from the 344th BS/98th BG at Yokota (*Roland T Speckman*)

so painted, post-haste. Ganey also requisitioned gun flash suppressors for the 0.50-cal guns aboard the Superfortresses, and ordered gunners to return fire. Lacking a satisfactory answer for the losses, he made it a part of the operational doctrine that future strike would be timed too coincide with adverse weather, which the B-29s could handle more readily than the MiGs.

It has long been understood that 'Black Tuesday' was the event that caused so much black paint to be applied to B-29s. But some crewmen remember the loss of three bombers on the Kwaksan Bridges raid as the final evidence that plenty of black paint was needed, without delay. Airman 2nd Class 'Bud' Farrell related;

'None of the 19th BG ships were painted black on the underbelly until 24 July 1952, and I believe it was due to the 19th BG having lost three ships on the night of 10 June over the Kwaksan Bridges, which was just before we arrived in the 19th on the 21st of that same month. Earlier daylight mission major losses of April and 23 October 1951 had not caused the painting of bottoms, but the loss of three B-29s to MiGs in full darkness, whilst coned in searchlights, required some new effort to suppress light reflection.

'On the morning of 24 July, I saw upon our arrival at the flightline to pre-flight our aircraft that several had been painted overnight, and this was just after the big Pyongyang raid of 11 July, when things were beginning to heat up again. Max effort missions were being planned to get the North Koreans/Chinese back to the truce talks at Panmunjom.'

In other units, B-29s that had had some black paint applied to their underfuselage area abruptly acquired 'wraparound' black schemes that engulfed the entire nose.

As the year progressed, FEAF Bomber Command approved raids against hydroelectric facilities, including dams, at Suiho, Fusen, Chosin and Kyosen. SHORAN-equipped B-29s were to attack during the night, while USAF and Navy fighter-bombers were to hit the same sites during the day. These attacks began on 24 June, and by the 27th it was estimated that 90 per cent of North Korean power supplies had been destroyed.

On 10 July FEAF issued a directive intended to wipe away the distinction between 'strategic' and 'tactical' targets, the USAF announcing that it was restructuring procedures for choosing and prioritising targets. The brass now believed there would be up to 80 targets per month for which SHORAN bombing would be appropriate. Fifth Air Force, which owned tactical air assets, had been better equipped to formulate target rosters than Bomber Command, which was sparsely populated in its intelligence shop. Now, Bomber Command acquired many new targets that had previously been assigned to fighter-bombers, but no new intelligence staff to analyse them. Much of the best information about targets in North Korea continued to be gleaned from photos taken by RB-29s of the 91st SRS.

11 July was the date chosen for massed tactical and strategic raids over North Korea, dubbed Operation *Pressure Pump*. The Superfortress

Seen from outside the Superfortress (as he might look when trying to spot an approaching MiG, except that the interior lights wouldn't be on), Airman 2nd Class Marcus E Padilla again sits at the left gunner's blister position, operating the remote control for his machine guns (*Roland T Speckman*)

portion of this effort saw 54 SHORAN-directed B-29s sent against eight targets. Although fighter-bombers and light bombers got good results during *Pressure Pump* – a one-day total of 1254 sorties – B-29 bombing accuracy remained poor.

Historian Robert Futrell described another problem faced by FEAF Bomber Command;

'Because of inaccuracies in existing Korean maps, all of Bomber Command's SHORAN targets had to be especially processed for attack by a multiplex stereo plotting process, which, in effect, justified maps against aerial mapping photography. In July 1952, the Far East Command's 64th Engineer Base Topographic Battalion could provide only five sets of multiplexed SHORAN coordinates a week. Early in July, FEAF air-targets people were so hard pressed to supply medium-bomber targets that they flatly stated that the North Korean transportation system was the "only target system suitable for B-29s in North Korea". FEAF Bomber Command accordingly used aircraft not scheduled for special targets in attacks against marshalling yards along the enemy's rail routes. These July marshalling yard attacks yielded pitifully small returns. Assessment of the results of nine missions involving 71 B-29 sorties showed only 17 rail cars destroyed or damaged.'

The Sungho-ri cement plant was the target of strikes by 44 Super-fortresses each on the nights of 19 and 21 July. Nine days later no fewer than 63 Superfortresses carried out a SHORAN raid against a metal-producing facility near Sinuiju in the largest B-29 effort against a single target during the war. The mission was purposely scheduled when weather was marginal near the target and undercast would confuse searchlights. Although MiG nightfighters appeared, they apparently never got close to the bombers. FEAF Bomber Command officials determined that the facility, which had been overlooked until now, was 90 per cent destroyed.

TARGETING DEBATE

Well into August 1952, even while targeting procedures were reconsidered, the limited multiplexing capability meant that B-29 missions yielded disappointing accuracy. Things began to improve the following month when the Air Force's 548th Reconnaissance Technical Squadron assembled a new multiplexing capability at Yokota. By year end the squadron could multiplex 90 targets per month, 'But we were never hitting fish in a pickle barrel, no matter what claims were made', remembered 1Lt Ned Smith, a 19th BG bombardier. 'We tried to bring together all the information we could muster and to achieve as much accuracy as possible, but it was nothing like the precision bombing of a later era'.

On 14 August 14 B-29s bombed the Nakwon munitions plant, said to be a manufacturer of anti-tank hand grenades. The bomb damage assessment was that the target was 60 per cent destroyed. However, Ganey was unhappy about being limited to marginal weather conditions by the searchlight, flak and MiG threat. As reported by historian Futrell, Ganey told FEAF commander Gen O P Weyland that he could put '60 B-29 aircraft within 1000 ft of any target within SHORAN range', and that 'to limit such a force to bad weather conditions indicates that targets remaining in North Korea are not suitable for medium bombing, or that the Air Force is at the mercy of a defensive tactic (long ago) discarded as

The arrival of the F-94B interceptor (the future C-model of which would be officially named the Starfire) was not initially of much help to B-29 Superfortress crews. The Pentagon considered the air intercept radar fitted in the nose of the F-94B to be so valuable that it did not want the fighter flying north of the bombline. This F-94B (51-5355) of the 319th Fighter Interceptor Squadron has just taken the arresting wire at K-13 Suwon Air Base, Korea (*Robert Dwan*)

outmoded'. Nevertheless, FEAF scheduled new attacks on hydroelectric facilities, as Futrell described it, 'when suitably bad weather promised to negate Red searchlight defences'.

The arrival of the F-94B nightfighter in 1952 was not initially of much help to B-29 crews. The Pentagon determined that the air intercept radar aboard the jet was so sensitive, there could be no risk of it falling into enemy hands. For weeks after its arrival, the F-94B was limited to operations south of the bombline, where the only enemy aircraft were Po-2 night intruders.

Superfortress crews might have been forgiven for wondering why the war was being fought this way. Their aircraft was older than bombers being flown by crews in the United States. Their principal defence against their foe, so far, consisted of black paint and bad weather. Bomb damage assessments kept reporting that certain targets were 60, 80 and 90 per cent destroyed, yet they kept going back to those targets again and again. All this time, fruitless armistice negotiations were dragging on. In a typical example of repetition, Superfortress crews flew yet more strikes against Pyongyang and the Suiho hydroelectric facility in September 1952. A few B-29s were now equipped with electronic jamming equipment, the reliability of which was in question, but otherwise little had changed.

On 19 September Superfortresses made a rare daylight sortie when 35 heavily escorted bombers attacked troop concentrations on the east coast of North Korea. Eight days later another somewhat atypical mission saw a dozen B-29s bomb railway bridges within North Korea. Results were disappointing.

The final attack of September occurred on the night of the 30th, when 45 Superfortresses mounted a maximum nocturnal effort against factories at Namsan-ni. It was a carefully coordinated raid, with B-26 Invaders harrying the foe near the target while the B-29s unloaded their bombs.

On 5 October Brig Gen William P Fisher replaced Brig Gen Wiley D Ganey as head of FEAF Bomber Command, which maintained its headquarters at Yokota. Responding to political developments in the distant background, where an armistice was being debated, Weyland asked Fisher to increase Bomber Command operations by 30 per cent, and to hit at least two targets per night between 9 and 18 October. The result was a major strain on B-29 crews.

As part of the lead up to this offensive, on 8 October ten B-29s of the 98th BG, escorted by Navy F2H-2 Banshees, used proximity-fused 500-lb bombs on a major North Korean railway junction that was

B-29s are marshalled out at the start of yet another bombing mission from Yokota in 1952 (*Roland T Speckman*)

Airman 2nd Class Frank 'Bud' Farrell in the rearward-facing left gunner's position of his B-29. He is sat opposite the astrodome where the remote control for his guns is located (*Frank Farrell*)

heavily defended by flak. An increase in tempo, and a joint effort with the Navy, were helpful to evolving doctrine, but to the men inside B-29 fuselages, the war seemed all too repetitive.

October saw Superfortresses flying nocturnal, radar-directed missions in support of friendly ground troops. Crews called these 'primer' missions, the strikes bolstering a much larger effort by FEAF fighter-bombers that were attacking Chinese troops near embattled hill positions with evocative names like 'Old Baldy', 'Sniper Ridge' and 'T-Bone Hill'. In addition to 'primer' missions, October also saw much of the Superfortress effort directed against communications and supply facilities.

Fisher was initially unhappy with the target list that he had inherited, and the ongoing discussion about targeting continued under the new Bomber Command boss. To Fisher, many of the so-called supply targets were simply villages and towns. He began to change his view, however, when bombs set off so many secondary fires and explosions that it was obvious the villages were arsenals. According to Futrell, Fisher believed these villages represented 'the last currently vulnerable link in the supply and distribution system of the Communist armies'.

The standard ordnance for both 'primer' and supply bombing raids was the 500-lb high-explosive bomb. FEAF boss Weyland wanted both the tactical aeroplanes of Fifth Air Force and the B-29s of Bomber Command to make greater use of incendiary munitions against supply targets. According to Futrell, Weyland felt that in the dry weather before the first snowfalls, the incendiaries would start fires that would feed on grass and brush and spread to dispersed ammunition dumps. While targeting and munitions were being debated, Superfortress crews continued 'primer' strikes in support of friendly ground troops.

On the 'primer' mission of 31 October, right gunner Airman 2nd Class Frank 'Bud' Farrell looked out at the raging seas near Okinawa as his bomber, *No Sweat II*, approached for a landing. 'Man, I'm glad we don't have to ditch in that', Farrell thought aloud, referring to sea condition. 'While the sky was clear as a bell with a very bright moon, the wind was very strong at surface level, and was piling up huge swells and waves, later reported as up to 20 ft, with surf – like white water for several miles out from the beach into the East China Sea. It was the roughest I had ever seen the waters off Okinawa'. Farrell doubted that a Superfortress crew could survive long enough to be rescued in such high seas.

Returning from the mission, behind Farrell's bomber, was 44-61751, a B-29-45BN Superfortress (c/n 11218) built by Boeing's Renton, Washington, factory. The crew called the aircraft *Lubricating Lady*, not because the name was painted on the nose, but because she had a long history of mechanical problems. 'She was the hangar queen of the 93rd BS/19th BG', said Farrell. 'We had taken her for test flights twice recently, and had mechanical problems both times'. 44-61751 apparently had not been touched by enemy action that night.

One of the crew members aboard *Lubricating Lady* was Airman 2nd Class Chuck Rees. 'I don't know whether flak hit us or not', Rees said in an interview. 'Nothing entered the aircraft. We didn't decompress. But on the way back from North Korea, we lost two engines about 90 miles from Okinawa. We called Air-Sea Rescue. They sent an SB-29 Superfortress rescue aircraft, which carries a lifeboat under its fuselage. Still, for a time we thought we would make it – until we lost a third engine'.

For ditching, two gunners in the rear fuselage were expected to crawl through the narrow tunnel above the B-29 bomb-bay and take up ditching positions in the forward part of the fuselage. 'The alarm bell rang', said Rees. 'The captain announced that we would ditch. We had some difficulty making it through the tunnel to reach our ditching position'.

Lubricating Lady went into the high seas. Later, when investigators pieced together what had happened, the bomber's pilot, Capt Robert G Harvey, and all of the crew's regularly assigned officers were dead. Right gunner Airman 2nd Class Donald Wilson lost his life, too, but only after a heroic effort. In the ditching position, he survived and was able to extricate himself from his astrodome, but he went back to help Chuck Rees, who was pinned in place by an item of equipment. Thrashing about in the cold, dark fuselage as it filled with water, Wilson extricated Rees, who went to the surface.

In the clear moonlight, helicopters, an SB-29 and an SA-16 Albatross were flying overhead. After about 90 minutes in the choppy, frigid seas, a crash boat arrived to rescue Rees, along with radio operator Airman 1st Class Edward B LeMaster and bombardier 1Lt James Knox. Not a regular member of *Lubricating Lady's* crew, Knox escaped through the nose.

'I was way under water, and the water was flooding in', Rees said later. 'I'm a Catholic, and I was saying the Act of Contrition when, suddenly,

An unsung hero of the 1950s was the Boeing's search and rescue aircraft with its 29-ft 9-in Edo A-3 lifeboat (being carried by the aircraft in the top photo only), which could be dropped from the air. An SB-17G Flying Fortress flew the very first air rescue mission of the Korean War, but from 25 June 1950 onward the SB-29 was available to rescue downed crews. The SB-29 retained all of its gun turrets, with the exception of the lower forward, which was replaced by a search radar (*US Air Force*)

hand grabbed me. I owe my life to Wilson', but Wilson was not around to celebrate. He went back to try to save another crew member and gave his own life.

The fate of 44-61751 remains something of a mystery. Rees and LeMaster were awarded the Air Medal almost 50 years after *Lubricating Lady* slipped beneath the waves, but Wilson has never received recognition. Veterans have been unable to locate Knox, who would be able to make a recommendation for an award.

As this B-29 formation heads for North Korea, an oil leak from the number two engine splatters black liquid on the left wing surface. The aircraft, from the 19th BS/93rd BG, is 44-61751, a B-29-45-BN Superfortress (c/n 11218) built at Boeing's Renton factory. The crew called the ill-fated Superfortress *Lubricating Lady* (*Frank Farrell*)

Farrell, who studied the mishap, said, 'The original report was that they had run out of fuel. But then the entire wing section of *Lubricating Lady* floated into Naha Harbour, Okinawa, and was retrieved. When they examined the wing, they found 600 gallons of fuel in the centre wing tank that could not, or would not, be transferred'. So why did 44-61751 go down? 'We may never know', said Farrell.

Rees continued, 'I think if it wasn't for Donald Wilson remaining on top of the aircraft, hanging on for dear life by clutching the four guns in the top turret and reaching back in to help those of us inside, I would not be alive today. Wilson may have had his head under water part of the time. There is some evidence that he may have taken off his life jacket and gone back into the aircraft to help others. He could have swum away and been rescued, yet he chose to help others'.

On the very day *Lubricating Lady's* aircraft commander, Capt Harvey, lost his life, his wife Mary Louise, in San Diego, California, gave birth to the couple's third child, a baby boy who was christened Clyde. Harvey had been a San Diego police officer since 1941, and had interrupted his work to fly the B-24 Liberator in World War 2, then resumed police work afterward. Like so many, he was recalled for duty in the Korean War.

In November 1952, Superfortress commanders turned to rescue forces – very effective throughout the war – and asked for a new precaution to be taken, in view of the increasing tendency of MiGs to stalk B-29s at night. They wanted the 37th Air Rescue Squadron (ARS) to sortie an SB-29 rescue aircraft, equipped with a 30-ft A-3 lifeboat, to follow closely behind the last B-29 bomber in every strike formation. The SB-29 crew would continuously monitor their radios so as to be available if a rescue attempt was needed. The rescue aircraft would follow the bombers to the Korean coast, then orbit at the point where they were expected to egress.

As it turned out, the SB-29s never used their rescue boats to help downed Superfortress crews, but they were ready to do so. Their presence was a morale booster.

NIGHTFIGHTERS

As late as November 1952, the Pentagon was still refusing to allow the USAF to fly its F-94Bs north of the bombline, but the Marine Corps had no such compunction about its radar-equipped F3D-2 Skyknights, which began operations that same month. Indeed, on 3 November a Skyknight crew was credited with the first jet-versus-jet aerial victory at night during the Korean War, and another Skyknight followed this success up when it claimed a MiG-15 at night five days later. By the end of the month, USAF chief of staff Gen Vandenberg had lifted the geographic restriction on the F-94B. Now, B-29 crews had available a constantly shifting protective screen formed by the F-94B and the F3D-2.

FEAF Bomber Command boss Fisher said the American nightfighters achieved 'some small degree of success' against the MiG threat, but noted that friendly radar sites were still not detecting the MiGs every time they came up. Tactics used by F-94B and F3D-2 crews were changed regularly to address this gap, and it was found that positioning a screen of F-94Bs and F3D-2s above a formation of B-29s deterred MiG attacks, which was, of course, the goal – but to the chagrin of pilots and radar observers, deterrence also reduced the prospects of scoring an aerial victory.

Trouble aplenty arose on a 6 November mission to bomb a supply centre at Unha-ri, which was defended by moderate flak. 1Lt Vernon R 'Bob' Hudder of the 344th BS/98th BG, who was navigator of a B-29 called *Hearts Desire II* (Wichita-built B-29 Superfortress 44-69656), wrote in his journal of a problem that happened all too often;

'On this mission, one of our photoflash bombs hung up in our bomb-bay. These were used to illuminate the target area for the camera in our aeroplane, and were time released after the regular bomb drop. Thus, our camera photos showed the location of our bomb strike in relation to the target. This indicated our crew's bombing accuracy.

'The first indication I had of a problem was when our new bombardier, Capt Grant Conant, moved quickly past my navigator's station, dropping his backpack parachute. At the same time, pilot, Capt Frank Riggs, announced the depressurisation of our cabin. With our crew already on oxygen, Conant opened the bomb-bay access door and, without his 'chute, but carrying an oxygen bottle, entered the bomb-bay and cut the wire holding the photoflash bomb. This occurred just seconds before our aircraft was lit up from the photoflash bomb going off – a close call.'

Hudder not only wrote a 'thank you' to bombardier Conant in his diary, he also bucked his gratitude a little higher up the chain. In the journal he cited Psalm 121:7: 'The Lord will keep you from all harm. He will watch over your life'.

Hudder would be expressing his thanks again within three weeks, as well as learning of the ability of the Superfortress to bring its crew home with two engines shot out. Years later he would say, 'I owe my life to the strength of that aeroplane'.

On 29 November the target was Sinuiju. Hudder had just finished R & R (rest and recuperation) leave to Tokyo and Yokohama. Some airmen called it 'I & I' (intoxication and intercourse), but not the devout Hudder. Of today's mission, he would later say, 'I could almost hear the brush of angel wings on this one. We encountered extremely intense flak, many searchlights and numerous MiGs.

The US Air Force categorised their B-29s as 'medium' bombers for political reasons during the Korean War – the Pentagon brass were locked in mortal combat arguing the merits of aircraft carriers versus B-36 bombers – but the mighty Superfortress still looked very much like a 'heavy' when taxiing out for a mission. These bombers of the 344th BS/98th BG are heading for the main runway at Yokota in the early evening for what would soon become a night mission
(*Roland T Speckman*)

'Our approach was from the west, over the Yellow Sea. The mission was a "max effort", with Okinawa-based B-29s. A very dramatic sight was Antung (the enemy's main MiG base in Manchuria) all lit up, with MiGs racing down the runway as they took off to climb up and challenge our bomber stream.

'Two of our engines were knocked out by flak over the target. Our aircraft had several holes and our tail section was damaged. One piece of shrapnel came up through the fuselage about two feet behind me and hit the Loran set. Well, I wouldn't be using that tonight!

'There was no way we could make it back to Yokota, so we headed for an emergency landing at K-8 Kunsan Air Base, in South Korea. A Marine Corps F3D-2 Skyknight nightfighter escorted us out of North Korea.

'As we were flying south, hoping to make it to South Korea, a popular song from World War 2 came to my mind – "Coming In On A Wing And A Prayer". The final words of the song are, "With our full crew aboard/and our trust in the Lord, we're coming in on a wing and a prayer". How appropriate!

'We landed in a blizzard with two engines out and a mountain at the south end of the runway (in reality, a hill about 200 ft high). There was no way for a "go-around". Capt Riggs performed an exceptional landing under the circumstances – I couldn't even see the ground until we touched down on the runway. That was a good example of why I was glad to fly with Riggs as my aircraft commander!'

MiG THREAT

As 1952 drew toward its end, intelligence officials determined that the Soviets now had two squadrons of MiG-15 nightfighters operating on a permanent basis just across the Yalu. The enemy had a highly developed ground control intercept (GCI) network, using ground radars and ground controllers to direct the MiGs aloft. The jets did not have an air intercept radar, however, so they were limited to radio and visual cues when they sought to engage the B-29s.

The Allies exploited the GCI network via secret listening posts on the island of Cho-do, sited off the coast of North Korea, and several other critical locations. These stations were manned by US Air Force language specialists, who monitored the enemy's communications. When everything was working right, the communists' own GCI transmissions could be intercepted and Superfortress crews warned that MiGs were heading for them.

'Blackbirds at rest' is the name photographer Russ Beard gave to this study of the hardstand at Kadena Air Base, where the 19th and 307th BGs were operating in late 1952. The compacted coral parking area extended up to the drinking water tank trailer (centre). The aircraft have had their tail fins completely covered in black paint to prevent searchlights from causing the vertical surface to flash, aiding nightfighters in their quest to spot the B-29s – the MiG pilots relied almost exclusively on visual acquisition of their targets. Bombs were normally stacked on both sides and at the back of each individual hardstand. When this photograph was taken the bomb pile was getting very low, although some ordnance can be seen below the tail of the B-29 in the foreground (*Russ Beard*)

Airmen 2nd Class Rex Parsons (right gunner) and Joe B Heacon (tail gunner) and Airman 1st Class Angelo Menna (central fire control gunner) gather at the right rear blister near the panel that divided the radar compartment from the gunners' compartment in the rear of the fuselage. They are flying in B-29-45-BN Superfortress 44-61751 (c/n 11218) *Lubricating Lady* **(***Frank Farrell***)**

Late in 1952, Brig Gen Fisher told his bosses that the B-29s were vulnerable to enemy defences, but that the bomber crews would operate with relative safety 'anywhere in North Korea except along the Yalu River'.

On 13 November, Weyland's interest in incendiaries came to the fore when five B-29s dropped clusters of firebombs on a supply site at Sopo, in North Korea. According to the subsequent battle damage estimate, the strike destroyed only 4.1 per cent of the target instead of the desired 60 per cent.

An unsung hero flying bombing missions during this period was Airman 1st Class Angelo Menna of the 93rd BS/19th BG. He was the central fire control (CFC) gunner on Wichita-built B-29-80-BW 44-70134 *No Sweat II*, which was piloted by Capt Brooke Cheney. A buddy of Menna's described the chaos that befell the Cheney crew that night;

'During our climb-out, approximately one hour out over the East China Sea from Okinawa, and ascending to bombing altitude as we headed for North Korea, we experienced a major, and almost catastrophic, malfunction of a gyro within our autopilot. This caused such a sudden dive of our aircraft that all loose equipment – floorboards, parachutes, life rafts and flak jackets – and unsecured crew members floated weightless to the top of the fuselage. We eventually crashed to the deck in a jumble upon pull-out of the dive by our aircraft commander, who had to manually override the malfunctioning autopilot.

'To make matters worse, the doors of the forward bomb-bay were open. We pulled out of an approximate 50-degree dive, far exceeding B-29 design limitations, at 1200 ft above the ocean, experiencing minor structural failure as rivets popped in the tail.

'In the sudden drop, our bomb load of 39 500-lb bombs and three photoflash bombs had floated weightless, hitting and denting the top of the racks, and leaving one 500 "pounder" hung at an angle and supported by only one lug on the shackle. The three photoflash bombs had come completely loose, with one (lying) on top of the hung 500 "pounder" and across the centre wing tank, and the other two rolling around on the latter, armed by the spinning propellers on their fuses.

'Angela Menna, our central fire control gunner, immediately checked the bomb-bay and saw the remaining hung bombs. Without hesitation, and without stopping to attach his chest pack parachute to his 'chute harness, Menna rushed into the rear bomb-bay, physically lifted the photoflash bombs and threw them out of the bay into the vast darkness and the ocean below. Finding the 500 "pounder" hung by one lug, he and Airman 2nd Class Rex Parsons – our right gunner – used a screwdriver to release the bombs, and then returned to the gunners' compartment.'

Another account of the same action includes this recollection;

'The aircraft commander told Rex to go in and help Angelo get the weight off the shackle hook so that he could use a screwdriver to trip the shackle. The aircraft commander told me to stand by at the bulkhead door, on interphone, with an Aldis lamp to give them light, and to report on their progress. When Rex was told to go into the open bomb-bay, he said, "Let's close that (bomb-bay) door first, if we can".

'Rex wore a backpack 'chute, and knew he could not fit between the bomb rack and the narrow crescent of the fuselage, so to reach the forward rack, he would have to swing out around the rear bomb rack and over the open bomb-bay doors, 200 miles out over a very black sea on a very black night. Angelo wore a chest pack harness but no 'chute pack, and could thus fit between the bomb rack and the fuselage.

'Fortunately, the doors did close, Rex went into the bomb-bay and helped, the aircraft commander opened the doors again, and the release was made. We headed back to Okinawa – the only airborne abort for this crew in the entire war. I felt a brief shudder when I realised how difficult it had been even to move against the centrifugal forces when I was sprawled on the deck under equipment, fighting to get up into a sitting position. I thought of a crew on an earlier mission, held prisoner in their fatal spin as they plunged for earth. It was very quiet on our aircraft for the remainder of our return flight, as though something critical might be further jarred loose by any talk, possibly jinxing our crew.'

The original account concludes, 'Angelo Menna's action, with absolutely no regard for his personal safety, in entering the bomb-bay and struggling with the bombs, deserve(s) recognition'. As this volume goes to press half a century after the Korean War, the US Air Force is now considering a belated award of the Distinguished Flying Cross to Menna.

MINE MISSION

On 17 November, Superfortresses attacked the remaining portion of a mine facility to the east of Sinuiju, and within sight of the Yalu, that had been struck earlier. The next day, they travelled to within 35 miles of the Yalu to attack the Songchon supply centre. The weather was clear and enemy aircraft succeeded in shooting down a B-29.

On the night of 19 November, according to accounts of the period, the enemy used a new approach to down a 98th BG Superfortress during a raid on a supply centre at Songchon, near the Yalu River. Flying high above an individual Superfortress (and out of its machine-gun range), a propeller-driven enemy aircraft – the type is not known – dropped flares each time the B-29 changed direction. The flares were used as a guide by searchlight crews, who then locked onto the bomber. Once the Superfortress was illuminated, MiGs appeared and opened fire. The tactic forced a bomber crew to bale out over Cho-do, giving the enemy another aerial victory.

In later years, crew members have questioned contemporary reports stating that the communists had dropped flares from above. Some veterans believe the enemy flares were actually friendly photoflash bombs from B-29s at higher altitude. Either way, the loss of a bomber that night was an especially tragic one.

'We dreaded the searchlights', said a 98th BG veteran who remembers that loss. 'They told us that the anti-aircraft batteries used by the Koreans and Chinese were German guns captured by the Russians in World War 2. The searchlights were radar controlled and were very good.

1Lt Archie T Booth was both a pilot and airborne electronic countermeasures (ECM) officer with the 307th BG. Before joining the Superfortress campaign over Korea, he had served as an enlisted sailor during World War 2, then joined the Army Air Corps and flown P-51 Mustangs in combat and T-6 Texan forward air control aircraft in the Korea War. There is no record of how he handled the B-29, but Booth once flew a T-6 down a street on a base below the roof level of a row of nearby warehouses (*Russ Beard*)

Col Charles B Westover, commander of the 98th Bombardment Wing at Yokota, presents the Distinguished Flying Cross to 1Lt Fred Traz following his actions in combat over North Korea. The officer to the right is the CO of Traz's 344th BS (*Roland T Speckman*)

And, of course, the German 88 mm gun was an exceptional weapon. That's why it was very important for our electronic countermeasures, or ECM, man to block the radars that controlled the lights and the guns'.

Among those lost on the 19 November shootdown was T/Sgt Morton Jensen, an ECM operator who was a legend in the B-29 community. Superfortress aircrew typically flew about 30 missions in a combat tour, but Jensen, who flew with various crews and squadrons within the 98th BG, was on his 100th mission that night. Reporters and photographers were waiting on the ground at Yokota to record his achievement as the first, and only, Superfortress crewmember to fly into enemy territory so many times. An official report, with minor editorial changes for easier reading, explains why the celebration for Jensen had to be cancelled;

'The B-29, aircraft 2173, piloted by Maj William F Sawyer, made a normal take-off. The approach to the initial point was made on the SHORAN arc as normal. Apart from a failure of the IFF package (information, friend or foe), the aircraft was in normal operating condition.

'The run-in to the target, made at 23,250 ft, was normal. Three flares were dropped in the path of the bomber, one at 5000 ft above and at nine o'clock, and two others above the aircraft at eleven o'clock (in the official report, they were flares dropped by an enemy aircraft – to crewmembers on the scene, they were errant American photoflash bombs). Sawyer later stated that ECM operator Jensen told him, "There are so many radars locked on us, I can't jam them all".

'After the flares burst, two searchlights came on and locked onto the B-29, followed very quickly by 15 to 20 more searchlights, which held the bomber in their beams for more than four minutes. 'There are too many frequencies', Jensen reported. At this point, a nightfighter fired four bursts, called "red watermelons" by a crewmember. They hit the number two engine. Two or more nightfighters were observed near the bomber.

'The tail gunner called out two aircraft at six o'clock high. More bursts of gunfire hit the number three engine. Hits were then received on the wing and fuselage. A fire was started and could not be put out. All crewmembers were on oxygen during the bomb run (even though the B-29 was pressurised, wearing oxygen during the bomb run was standard procedure). The searchlights went away from the B-29 and the aircraft commander called Dutch Boy (apparently the radio call sign for the US command post on the island of Cho-do, off the coast of North Korea), using Dog Channel (the emergency radio frequency). Dutch Boy directed a 200-degree heading, soon adjusted to a 220-degree heading. At this point the aircraft was burning, and was dropping at a rate of 500 ft per minute while at a speed of 280 miles per hour.

'When the bomber was ten miles north-west of Chinampo a third heading of 236 degrees was ordered. Ever since being hit, the crew had begun bale-out procedure. It was determined that there was not sufficient time to take off the parachute harness, slip into the exposure suit and put the parachute harness back on.

'Aircraft commander Sawyer ordered the crew to bale out. The aft door was opened and tied back, the bomb-bay doors were opened and the nose wheel was lowered to facilitate exit through the nose wheel well. Sawyer gave the bale-out order verbally and by ringing the alarm bell. The crew began baling out at 2800 ft. The aircraft turned slowly to the left and went

Loading up again, gunners from the 344th BS/98th BG pose for an official USAF photograph at Yokota in late 1952 (*Roland T Speckman*)

into the water near Cho-do Island. After receiving an interphone call from the last man in the rear fuselage saying he was leaving, Sawyer got out of his seat, stepped over the crash bar, climbed down the rungs on the side of nose wheel well and let go.

'Once free of the aircraft, he pulled the ripcord. His parachute opened normally with no perceptible shock. He observed a flare one and one-half miles north of him. He hit the ground on Cho-do Island backward on the side of a hill and was lowered to a prone position on his back. He rolled over, collapsed his 'chute and got out of his harness. He saw lights glowing to the north of him. He walked into that direction and encountered a South Korean Marine, who said, "Yes, there are Americans nearby", then walked away and left him standing there. Sawyer eventually reached the US command post on Cho-do.

'1Lt Allan R Winchester, the radar operator, experienced a similar bale-out. He went through the aft pressure door, stood by the escape hatch in the crouched position with arms stretched out, jumped into the night and pulled his rip cord. He observed other parachutes. When he touched down, he simply sat down in the water near Cho-do Island. Winchester had difficulty getting untangled, wriggled out from his 'chute, inflated his dinghy, covered himself with a poncho and was able to use a single paddle. A sampan from Cho-do picked him up after seven hours in the water. Though not wearing his exposure suit, Winchester wore long winter underwear, coveralls and an L-2 flying jacket, all of which probably contributed to his survival in the elements.'

There were 14 men on the B-29, including ECM operator Jensen, who was never heard from again and never confirmed to be captured (although some of the crew apparently did come down on the mainland, in enemy territory). The remains of two were retrieved near Cho-do where the two survivors ended up. The other ten B-29 crewmembers have never been satisfactorily accounted for. There have been reports that one of them was captured and shot on the scene.

The difficult situation with enemy flares, searchlights, and nightfighters became even worse on the night of 30 December. With a full moon illuminating them from above and contrails streaming back at bomber altitudes, three 19th BG Superfortresses were caught by searchlights whilst on a raid near the Yalu. A propeller-driven enemy aircraft is reported to have radioed the bombers' whereabouts while flying above them. MiGs shot down one B-29 and damaged the remaining two so badly that they had to divert to airfields in South Korea.

The moonlight and the ambient temperature were not really to blame, for as the third calendar year of the Korean War drew to a close, the enemy was improving his air defence capabilities.

1953

'Equal doses of danger and drudgery' said one B-29 crewmember about the Korean War as it entered its fourth calendar year (and 31st month). At the beginning, there had been a sense of newness and adventure to the whole thing. When the MiG-15 appeared, the mood blackened. It never got better, but an element of dreariness soon joined the feeling of gloom – Superfortress crews were up against lethal defences, and there was nothing new or adventurous about any of it.

On the night of 4 January 1953, a dozen B-29s of the 307th BW bombed the Huichon supply areas and railway bridge. Five nights later 17 Superfortresses began a new campaign against the Sinanju communications complex by bombing railway bridges at Yongmi-dong, anti-aircraft gun positions near Sinanju and two marshalling yards at Yongmi-dong and Maejung-dong. Fighter-bombers made follow-up strikes against those targets 24 hours later, while 307th BW B-29s bombed Sonchon and Anju marshalling yards. One of the bombers was caught in the glare of searchlights after the foe observed its contrails, allowing a MiG to dive out of the darkness and shoot it down. It was an especially gruesome and unpleasant loss, for the crew of another B-29 was able to see pieces of the bomber falling like shards of silver in the shifting glare of the searchlights.

LEAFLET DROP

Very late in the Korean era (beginning in January 1953), the USAF created, equipped and trained the 580th, 581st and 582d Air Resupply and Communication Wings (ARCWs) for unconventional warfare. According to the book *Apollo's Warriors* by Col Michael E Haas, the job of the B-29s belonging to these units was to deliver 'Ranger-type personnel and their supplies deep behind the Iron Curtain'. In his volume, which is subtitled *US Air Force Special Operations During the Cold War*, Haas writes about the difficulties of adapting the B-29 for behind-the-lines work;

'The Superfortress was not a happy choice for the service, which noted the limitations of using a high-speed, high-altitude bomber for low-speed, low-level night infiltration missions. Modifications included removing all guns for self-defence, saving those in the tail turret, and installing a "joe hole" in the former aft belly turret space for parachutists to exit. Resupply bundles would hang like clusters of melons in the bomb-bay to be dropped like bombs as the aeroplane passed over the drop zone.'

The special units also tested an apparatus designed to snatch up a person from the ground and reel him into the aircraft. In one test at a stateside base, the system was used to pick up a test pig in a small cage. The arrangement was eventually dropped, although it would re-appear in later wars as the Fulton recovery system.

The special units stood up and operated with relatively inexperienced B-29 crews, the 580th forming at Mountain Home Air Force Base, Idaho, the 581st at Clark Field, the Philippines, and the 582nd at Wheelus Field, Libya. In unusual secrecy, they operated B-29s, C-47s,

SA-16s and helicopters, and took their orders from USAF offices in an unmarked office building on Wisconsin Avenue, in Washington DC.

Indeed, so secret were the ARCWs that when a 581st H-19 helicopter rescued top ace Capt Joe McConnell after his F-86 went down in the Yellow Sea, the USAF re-enacted the rescue at a lake in Japan to create a much-published photo that gave the impression McConnell had been picked up by the Air Rescue Service. rather than the clandestine unit.

On 15 January, MiG-15s guided by radar-controlled searchlights intercepted a solitary B-29 known as 'Stardust 40', piloted by Capt Wallace L Brown, but also with the 581st ARCW's commander, Col John K Arnold Jr, on board. MiGs and the Superfortress converged just 12 miles south of the Yalu River at 2330 hrs, and within moments, three of the bomber's four engines were on fire.

In Robert Futrell's official history of the USAF in Korea, the aircraft was an RB-29 of the 91st SRS, and the action took place on 12 January 'in the dark skies above North Korea'. Futrell could not have known otherwise. In fact, the B-29 (it was not an RB-29) was one of four belonging to the 581st ARCW, but detailed to the 91st SRS for leaflet-drop duty. The primary job of the 581st ARCW was to drop agents behind the lines in both North Korea and China for the Central Intelligence Agency. The lost Superfortress apparently went down not over North Korea but only after straying into Manchuria. The crew of nine was captured, and the Chinese horribly mistreated the men and put them through a highly publicised propaganda trial after the Korean War. China detained the men for two-

Below
B-29 Superfortresses of the 98th BG sit side-by-side on the vast Yokota apron, ready for their next combat mission in 1953
(*Roland T Speckman*)

Bottom
The haste in which the black paint was applied to the undersurfaces of the 98th BG's B-29s is clearly evident in this close up view of a 344th BS machine in 1953
(*Roland T Speckman*)

and-a-half years before their eventual (and secret) release. Arnold was the second highest-ranking American to be taken prisoner during the war, junior only to a colonel from an RB-45C Tornado crew.

The relatively high altitude leaflet drop by the 581st ARCW should have been safer than the low-level agent drops that were the unit's speciality. Ironically, although many dozens of these missions were flown in what the US military calls 'psychological operations,' often abbreviated as 'psyops', a study near the end of the Korean War suggested that the leaflets were useless, or even counterproductive. Far from per-suading enemy troops to surrender, according to the study, the 'psyops' leaflets often hardened the foe's determination.

MOON, MiGS

On the night of 28 January the glow of a full moon illuminated a B-29 for the enemy, and MiGs duly shot

Roland T Speckman, 'Speck' to his friends, flew the C-87 Liberator Express in World War 2, the B-29 Superfortress in Korea and the HH-43F Huskie helicopter in Vietnam. He was a first lieutenant when this 1953 portrait of a B-29 pilot at work was snapped. His unit was the 344th BS/98th BG at Yokota. 'Speck' retired with the rank of lieutenant colonel (*Roland T Speckman*)

'Speck' T Speckman poses in front of the sign at the headquarters of the 344th BS at Yokota. The unit was nicknamed the 'Eliminators' (*Roland T Speckman*)

it down. This was the fourth B-29 to be lost to enemy action in less than a month, a stunning blow to FEAF Bomber Command. Viewed in retrospect, one positive note is that this was the final Superfortress combat loss of the Korean War, even though the conflict would continue for further six months.

On the night of 30 January, no fewer than ten enemy fighters attacked a B-29 and damaged it badly enough to force an emergency landing in South Korea.

'That was a tough night', remembered 1Lt Vernon R 'Bob' Hudder of the 344th BS/98th BG, the navigator of Wichita-built B-29 44-69656 *Hearts Desire II*. Hudder wrote in his journal than 30 January was supposed to be a piece of cake;

'Our target was a supply arsenal on the main supply route from Manchuria to the frontline. It was located near Wonsan, the harbor city on the east coast which was usually considered to be a milk run.

'A funny thing happened on this mission. Figuring nothing exciting ever occurred over Wonsan, they put a civilian passenger on board – a "wheel" from FEAF Bomber Command who was going back to the US. He wanted to know what a bombing mission was like, as long as it wasn't a "hot" target. Soon after coasting into South Korea, we headed up the east coast toward Wonsan, and received reports from our GCI (ground control intercept) of "bandits" (MiGs) in the air. As I plotted the grid locations of the "bandits" on my map, our passenger who sat on the nose wheel access door near my station repeatedly scrutinised my actions.

'Closer and closer, the MiGs were approaching our bomber stream and our passenger grew obviously more concerned. "I thought nothing exciting ever happened over Wonsan. That's what they told me at FEAF headquarters", he stated with a quiver in his voice.

'"Usually it is quiet over Wonsan. Maybe the communists heard you were riding with us tonight!" I said with a grin. As it turned out, we dropped our bomb load as the "Lead" aircraft and exited North Korea just as the MiGs arrived in the target area. Later, the MiGs fired on bombers in our stream.

'The mission was a huge success. We destroyed 70 buildings and started huge fires in the target complex, and our passenger had a "war story" to relate when he arrived back in the States!'

By the time of this mission, the procedures for night sorties over North Korea were pretty thoroughly established. One crewmember said that the hardest time was taxiing out for a mission, wondering whether, a few hours later, he would be taxiing back. Hudder described the procedures in his memoir:

'All aircraft scheduled for the mission would taxi to the end of the runway, lined up in the order of their position in the bomber stream. Takeoff rolls began at one-minute intervals, the "hack" given by the navigator precisely on the second hand reaching the minute mark. All navigators' watches were synchronised during the mission briefing.

'After taking off from Yokota, the bomber stream followed the same route departing Japan for Korea (roughly south past Tokyo, then north-west across Japan and north over the sea toward Korea). The bomber stream crossed the Sea of Japan and coasted into South Korea at various locations, depending on our target area in North Korea.

'Our return to Yokota also followed a set route, entering Japan at Shishizu, proceeding to a homing beacon and entering the landing pattern for our home base. The fuel supply was usually low on arrival at Yokota, especially if we encountered a jetstream over North Korea.

'Bomber stream attacks always followed a pattern. Arrival over the CP (control point) at the scheduled time was important. Aircraft spacing was one minute apart over the CP, thus our usually scheduled 12 B-29s would be in and out of the target area in 12 minutes. When FEAF Bomber Command scheduled a "max effort", as many as 60 B-29s could be involved, including B-29s from the two wings based on Okinawa.

'After giving their time over the CP, the aircraft proceeded to the IP (initial point). This was the start of the bomb run, and from this point the radar observer directed the aircraft along the SHORAN arc to the target. Each B-29 announced its time over the IP, maintaining the one minute spacing. Once over the IP, my duties as navigator ended and the radar observer took over for the SHORAN bomb run. My next duty was to recite the exact time of our "bombs away".

'Immediately after the IP, I would recite the part of Psalm 23 that says, "Ye though I walk through the valley of death, I will fear no evil". On the bomb run, I would position my desk lamp down to the table in order to shut out its light. Then, I could pull back the black curtain over the window to my left and observe the action taking place outside.

'Upon release of our bombs, I gave the new heading to the aircraft commander and prepared the strike report, which was called in to FEAF Bomber Command.

'Departing Korea, I would shoot at least one celestial fix (two if possible) en route back to Japan. To "shoot" the stars, I had to climb up and sit under the astrodome, located at the forward end of the tunnel that went from the front of our B-29 to the rear, over the bomb-bay.

'On several occasions, astrodomes blew out. The suction was so great that it stripped the quilted lining from the entire tunnel. To prevent navigators from being sucked out of the hole, it was important to "lock"

En route to a target deep in enemy territory – this was the view from the bombardier's perch (*Roland T Speckman*)

yourself in when taking celestial shots. For this reason, navigators were required to wear a chest parachute with harness. Because the parachute was too bulky to wear in the tunnel, it was removed and the harness clips were fastened to the fittings of the tunnel. This would keep us from being sucked out of the aircraft if the astrodome did indeed blow out.

'On every mission, I made it a point to arrive in the astrodome early enough to observe the heavens and to locate the stars I planned to shoot.

'Landing at Yokota was sometimes interesting. Fuel was always a factor, as weather conditions could be severe (heavy snow or fog). After landing, we parked and vacated our aeroplane and proceeded to the squadron debriefing room for mission summary. This completed the mission.'

Elsewhere in his memoir, Hudder wrote that the weather was as much a problem as the enemy. B-29 crews were constantly battling jetstreams, snow and fog. 'Over Korea, the outside temperatures at altitude ranged to 60 degrees below zero Fahrenheit. In order to keep warm, I wore "long johns" under my winter flying suit. In addition, I wore winter padded pants and a winter flying jacket, with a hood. On the front of the hood was wolf hair that hung in front of my face and became icy at altitude. While we were descending, the ice would thaw and drip. Two pairs of heavy socks under jump boots helped keep my feet warm, but on really cold nights I also wore padded flying boots. And I would still be cold!'

SEARCHLIGHTS, FLAK, MiGS

On the very night Hudder was entertaining a civilian on a B-29 flight to Wonsan (30 January), the F-94B crew of Capt Ben L Fithian and 1Lt Sam R Lyons downed a Lavochkin La-9 in the first aerial victory to be claimed at night by a USAF fighter. F-94Bs and Marine Corps F3D-2s continued to evolve tactics aimed at protecting the B-29 force. They had one small advantage – unlike the MiGs, they had air-to-air radar. In some cases the mere appearance of an F-94B or F3D-2 would turn back formations of MiGs, but the threat to B-29 crews remained very real.

Brig Gen William P Fisher, commander of FEAF Bomber Command, tirelessly scrutinised the reasons why a relatively modest effort by the enemy was achieving lethal results against his bombers. A staff committee reminder Fisher of the obvious – SHORAN bombing required crews to follow a prescribed flightpath, which rendered Superfortresses vulnerable to enemy anti-aircraft fire. The Soviets, Chinese and North Koreans understood SHORAN, and concentrated their defences along the routes bombers would follow to their targets.

Futrell described Fisher's decision processes as a result of these losses;

'Fisher ordered his B-29 commanders to cut the time required to attack a target by SHORAN to the absolute minimum. On one occasion, for example, the B-29 stream had been over Namsan-ni for two hours, and the Reds had been able to give undivided attention to each individual bomber. As a matter of highest precedence, Bomber Command emphasised the compression of its bomber streams so that individual bomber crews would attack at one-minute instead of three-minute intervals. Whenever possible, the bombers were assigned as many as four separate SHORAN aiming points, so that the crews could attack as nearly simultaneously as possible. By such procedures, as many as nine strike aircraft could be in a space 1000 ft wide and eight miles long, each giving mutual support to the other.

A 98th BG B-29 heads north along an unidentified river as it approaches its target in North Korea (*Roland T Speckman*)

Bomber Command's compression tactics received continuous emphasis, and FEAF reported that "maximum compression of the B-29 force was the outstanding device for reducing overall risk".'

Futrell also quoted Fisher in respect to the MiG's lack of radar;

'If the Communists ever crack that last link and get an all-weather capability of pressing an accurate firing attack, the B-29 business is really going to get rough.'

Concerns about the vulnerability of the B-29 to searchlights, flak and MiGs were so serious that in late January, Fisher and other leaders were seriously discussing the prospect of retiring the Superfortress from duty. This discussion went ahead even though the Pentagon was offering no prospect that any other bomber (B-36, B-47 or B-50) would be committed to battle in Korea. As it happened, the discussion was taking place at the wrong time, for no further B-29s were lost as a result of enemy action.

At the end of January, FEAF Bomber Command reported that interceptions by MiGs had resulted in 23 firing passes against Superfortress formations. The toll of four B-29s lost included 'Stardust 40'.

FEBRUARY 1953

Superfortress crews flew both frontline support missions and strikes deep into North Korea in the second month of the year while armistice negotiators continued to haggle. Navigator Hudder remembers a mission to the North Korean capital, Pyongyang, on the night of 14 February, when the target 'was an underground communications/radio station, protected by 12 feet of reinforced concrete. For this mission we carried eight 2000-lb armour-piercing bombs, with steel heads.

'Only eight crews participated in this mission – four from our 98th BW and four from the Okinawa-based 19th BW. Instead of our normal altitude separation of 500 ft, we maintained an altitude separation of 200 ft, and the average altitude over the target was 20,000 ft. Most bombing altitudes during our tour were between 18,000 and 26,000 ft. We ran into heavy flak and encountered many searchlights but, praise the Lord, we came through unscathed.'

On 21 March, as part of a larger FEAF combat effort dubbed *Spring Thaw*, 18 B-29s bombed three bridges at Yongmi-dong, and were credited with taking down two of them. When next they returned to this target, eight Superfortress crews found construction work on the severed spans almost complete. FEAF Bomber Command subsequently determined that flak defences around Yongmi-dong were so intense that it was not worth the risk to send Superfortresses against the bridges a third time.

On the nights of 6, 7 and 11 April, in a repeat of *Spring Thaw* but without the name, B-29s struck the three serviceable railway bridges across

The blackened exteriors of these Superfortresses, seen late in the Korean War, gives them an ominous appearance as the 344th BS/98th BG prepares to depart Yokota to attack a target in North Korea (*US Air Force*)

the Chongchon River at Sinanju. Although the bombers again severed spans, the enemy was observed to begin repairs immediately.

Large, lucrative targets were becoming fewer and fewer as tactical aeroplanes, carrier-based jets, B-26s and B-29s ranged over North Korea. Partly in the belief that it would help to advance armistice negotiations, on the night of 18 May, 18 B-29s attacked military installations at Sinuiju that had previously been hit by F-84s.

The following night, 14 B-29s bombed a military complex near Sinanju and were credited with destroying 117 buildings. The site was regarded as a key resupply point that would be used by the foe to move new units into North Korea on the eve of any armistice. Increasingly, the selection of B-29 targets would be aimed at preventing an enemy build-up in the event of a cease-fire.

A B-29 Superfortress crew of the 343rd BS/98th BG is issued hot coffee, spiked with an ounce of whiskey, at Yokota following the completion of yet another bombing mission (*Roland T Speckman*)

One of the last major targets for the B-29 in the Korean War was the Kuwonga Dam, just north of Pyongyang – one of several irrigation dams attacked in the hope of speeding up armistice talks. After fighter-bombers worked the place over for days, on the night of 21 May seven B-29s struck it with 56 2000-lb bombs. They had little effect, in part because the North Koreans had lowered the water level behind the dam, decreasing the pressure on it. A second visit in late May also failed to breach the dam.

May also saw B-29s fly 35 strikes against supply areas and troop billets – especially those that might strengthen the enemy on the eve of a cease-fire. On the night of 7 June, 14 bombers returned to a likely enemy resupply point near Sinanju, and were credited with destroying 250 buildings.

At the start of June 1953, the threat of a Chinese offensive on the ground was a huge distraction. The enemy was jockeying for position in the knowledge that truce talks would soon lead to an agreement to end the fighting along existing battle lines. On the nights of the 3rd, 4th and 5th, 19 B-29s flew ground radar-directed sorties against Chinese troop concentrations. As the month progressed, and further missions were flown in direct support of frontline troops, air liaison officers on the ground with the 502nd Tactical Control Group (who normally controlled tactical aeroplanes), took charge of guiding B-29s to their drop points.

On 15 June, Brig Gen Richard H Carmichael replaced Fisher as head of FEAF Bomber Command. 'I was surprised to find him there', remembered Col Ancil Baker, a B-29 pilot who arrived several months later. 'Carmichael had been a prisoner of the Japanese during World War 2, and had been badly abused. But as he settled into his duties at Yokota, just outside Tokyo, he denied any animosity toward the Japanese and did not appear to be in the least bit vindictive – a truly professional military man'. Carmichael was also a former commander of the 98th BG.

Throughout 1953, the two wings on Okinawa (19th and 307th BWs) and the one at Yokota (98th BW) were each authorised 31 Superfortresses,

plus two spares, meaning that FEAF was authorised 99 B-29s. Technically, the 98th and 307th BWs still belonged to SAC, while the 19th BW was a kind of permanent resident in the region, and reported to Twentieth Air Force. Historian Futrell described the difference as follows;

'The 19th Group was not organised according to SAC principles and, as a matter of fact, still used the old crewchief maintenance system whereby a single assigned crew maintained a single aircraft. Other factors were partly to blame, but the 19th's aircraft-in-commission rate declined and dragged FEAF Bomber Command's rate below the 70 per cent of aircraft-in-commission mark which was desirable.'

An extensive reorganisation of the 19th BG took place over a period of some months, concluding at the start of June, creating the 19th BW. In addition, the 19th was given an opportunity to rotate older B-29s to the US, replacing them with less war-weary Superfortresses.

In another reorganisation that concluded in June 1953, FEAF Bomber Command established a detachment at Itazuke Air Base, in western Japan. The unit would handle servicing and maintenance of Okinawa-based B-29s that suffered battle damage and were forced to divert to bases in South Korea or Japan. Previously, it had been necessary to despatch maintenance crews on an ad hoc basis every time a damaged B-29 diverted to Kimpo or Itazuke. The precaution was viewed by some as taking place 36 months later than it should have done.

The emphasis was now on airfields and bridges in North Korea. The objective was to keep these fields unserviceable, since tentative truce terms being negotiated at Panmunjom would allow for a 12-hour

44-86316 receives attention between sorties on the 98th BG apron at Yokota in 1953. This particular B-29 was manufactured by the Glenn L Martin Company of Omaha, Nebraska (*Roland T Speckman*)

Opposite page
This series of photographs shows 98th BG crews loading and then checking bombs at Yokota in early 1953 (*Roland T Speckman*)

free period between the signing of the truce agreement and the time it would become effective, giving the communists enough time to move in massive numbers of aircraft to the ten major North Korean airfields.

ARMISTICE TALKS

By July 1953, it was increasingly clear that armistice talks were moving toward a settlement. Chinese troops were fighting for new ground in the expectation they would keep it at the time of a cease-fire. Thus, soldiers fought brutal battles for valueless pieces of real estate like Pork Chop Hill and Bloody Ridge. Superfortresses, increasingly directed by tactical controllers, began dropping air burst 4000-lb bombs, which were deemed highly effective against ground troops.

During the period 13 through 19 July, Superfortresses flew 100 night sorties in direct support of ground troops. That month also saw heavy B-29 activity directed against airfields in North Korea. Repeated visits were made to the main airport in the capital Pyongyang, first with 100-lb bombs and later with 500 'pounders'. Other night strikes were directed against airfields at Namsi, Taechon, Hwangju, and Sinanju.

This activity continued after 29 July when UN Command boss Gen Mark Clark told FEAF CO Weyland that an armistice was imminent. Bomber Command boss Carmichael despatched a final wave of B-29 raids against airfields that he called a 'blaze of glory'. FEAF intelligence experts reported the enemy was moving MiGs across the Yalu to Uiju airfield, and Carmichael's crews were credited with destroying 21 jets on the ground. In the hope of destroying more, F-84s followed the B-29s to Uiju and worked over the airfield with bombs and strafing runs.

On 27 July 1953, at 1000 hrs, negotiators for the three armies in the field – the UN Command, the Korean Peoples Army and the Chinese Peoples Volunteers – met at Panmunjom to sign a cease-fire agreement.

In 37 months of conflict, more than a million human beings had perished. The US suffered 33,652 battle deaths, 3262 other deaths and 103,284 wounded. These are the current Pentagon figures, which have been adjusted in recent years.

Numerous key players, including South Korea's President Syngman Rhee, resisted the armistice, which remains in effect today. No government has ever signed it. In fact, Rhee abandoned active resistance only when the United States offered him a mutual defence treaty. Signed the following year, it too remains in effect today, and commits the US to the defence of South Korea if it is attacked.

Mission accomplished. Passing behind a 40 mm Bofors anti-aircraft gun manned by US Army soldiers (and never fired in anger), a black-garbed B-29 Superfortress of the 98th BW settles in for a landing at Yokota just before the end of the Korean War on 27 July 1953 (*US Air Force*)

There has never been a peace agreement to supplant the cease-fire. Chinese forces withdrew from Korea, and from the armistice process, soon afterwards, but the UN Command and the Korean Peoples Army continue to meet at Panmunjom in the 21st century, still administering a cease-fire that has never been followed by an official end to the Korean War.

Clark, who authorised signing of the armistice for the UN Command, called the Korean armistice 'the most distasteful moment of my life'. The actual signing of the armistice was done by Maj Gen William K Harrison Jr, and by that now-familiar martinet Gen Nam Il for both the North Korean and Chinese armies. Although the Allies achieved what they set forth to accomplish in Korea – assure the survival of South Korea after it came under attack – many viewed the Korean War as a failure, as well as a ratcheting up of the Cold War.

Historian Futrell noted that the armistice 'marked the attainment of UN and US military objectives in Korea'. At the time, few shared the bitterness of Clark, who said, 'I cannot bring myself to exalt at this hour'. He meant 'exult', but many Americans were doing exactly that, feeling the war was a success.

WAR'S END

The war ended for B-29 crews. For most, it came as an anticlimax. Airman 2nd Class Chuck Rees of the 93rd BS/19th BG – one of three survivors in a Superfortress ditching that claimed 11 lives, and who went on to fly five more combat missions after the ditching – came home to his mother's house in Darby, Pennsylvania, to find that the Air Force had sent him a bill

Tail gunner Airman 1st Class Kenneth Roberts of the 344th BS/98th BG looks out from the relatively roomy station operated by the crew member farthest aft in the Superfortress (*Roland T Speckman*)

for over $800 for the parachute, life vest, 0.45-cal pistol and other items that had not been returned to his unit's supply sergeant following the ditching. It seemed a poor way to thank Rees for his service. Rees sent a letter back to the Air Force explaining patiently that he had turned in all government-issue items with the exception of a few that lay at the bottom of the sea inside a flooded B-29 with dead Americans on board. 'They never replied and they never sent me a bill again', Rees said.

Capt Frederick Newman, a navigator on one of the last B-29 missions of the war, remembers that, 'Nobody wanted to be the last man to die in Korea. There was a definite feeling that everything had grown old and

The first air refuellings on a combat mission took place during the Korean War, and involved KB-29P tankers of the 43rd Air Refueling Squadron using a probe and drogue system. They were joined in the combat zone soon after the Korean Armistice by KB-29M models (shown here), which had been converted into aerial tankers at Boeing's Wichita, Kansas, plant. The conversion removed all gun turrets and bombing equipment, and saw the installation of a 2300-gallon jettisonable fuel tank in both bomb bays. Fuel lines were then routed to a 200-ft hose on a drum that was reeled out of the tanker by a steel cable from the receiver aircraft (US Navy)

tired, that there was not much left to bomb anyway, and that it was time to go home'. Newman added that, 'Some of our B-29s were relatively low-hour aeroplanes, having been swapped out for examples that were war-weary. But some of them were real dogs, and would not have been able to keep flying much longer'.

B-29 pilot Col Ancil Baker, who arrived too late to participate in the fighting, discovered that even after the armistice, Korea was considered a combat zone for tax purposes. 'For flying over Korea at least once a month, crews were still authorised to deduct $ 200 per month from gross income on their federal income tax returns. In my case, it amounted to a saving to $36 per month'. Baker also found that even when the enemy was not shooting, things could get hairy;

'I aged a couple of years when, returning from a night mission, my tail gunner lost his oxygen. Getting back to that position with a walk-around bottle of oxygen is not easy. Fortunately, we were coming home from the north, where there were no more mountains between us. From 20,000 ft, I headed for the ground as fast as I could without freezing the engines and losing turbo-supercharging. I radioed an emergency to Yokota, and they brought me straight in and met us with an ambulance. I was happy that no damage was done. I hope that tail gunner is well and happy today.'

In the final days of the war, and for months afterwards, crews were split up and individuals sent home separately. The B-29 remained in the Far East until 1955, and it was joined in 1954 by the first KB-29 tankers to be permanently assigned to the region. In 1955, entire units began to replace their Superfortresses, which was the year picked by the US Congress as the official end of the Korean War for pay and decoration purposes.

By war's end, B-29s had flown 21,000 sorties and dropped 167,000 tons of bombs. Thirty-four had been lost in combat (16 to fighters, four to flak and 14 to other causes), and B-29 gunners had been credited with destroying 27 enemy fighters (including 16 MiG-15s) and probably destroying 17 more (all MiG-15s). A further 11 aircraft had been damaged (all MiG-15s again).

As the Korean War dragged on and the MiG threat became greater, B-29s became blacker and blacker. A magnifying glass would be necessary to see the five red MiG-15 silhouettes painted against the black surface just below the pilot's position, COMMAND DECISION having been credited with five MiGs. It is, however, unlikely that any B-29 crew really shot down that number of communist fighters. Wichita-built B-29-85-BW Superfortress 44-87657 had served in the 99th BG during World War 2 and in the 19th BG during the Korean conflict. Capt Donald M Kovic and his crew flew COMMAND DECISION for a considerable period of time in 1953 (US Air Force)

Despite its age and vulnerability, the Superfortress had once again proven itself as an effective weapon of war. Indeed, post-war statistics reveal that B-29 losses worked out at less than one per 1000 sorties.

APPENDICES

B-29 UNITS OF THE KOREAN WAR

Far East Air Forces (FEAF)
FEAF Bomber Command
Twentieth Air Force, Kadena Air Base, Okinawa

19th Bombardment Group (Medium)
Kadena Air Base, Okinawa
June 1950 to May 1954
28th Bombardment Squadron (Medium) - 'Indian' emblem (green)
30th Bombardment Squadron (Medium) -'Finnegan the Cop' emblem (blue)
93rd Bombardment Squadron (Medium) - 'Screaming Indian' emblem (red)

Strategic Air Command
FEAF Bomber Command

31st Strategic Reconnaissance Squadron (Very Long Range) (Circle X)
Kadena Air Base, Okinawa
25 June to 16 November 1950 (redesignated 91st SRS on latter date)

22nd Bombardment Group (Medium) 'Red Raiders' (Circle E)
Kadena Air Base, Okinawa
July to October 1950
2nd Bombardment Squadron (Medium) (red)
19th Bombardment Squadron (Medium) (blue)
33rd Bombardment Squadron (Medium) (yellow)

92nd Bombardment Group (Medium) 'Alley Oop' (Circle W)
Yokota Air Base, Japan,
8/9 July to 25 October 1950 (then to Spokane, Washington, to convert to B-36)
325th Bombardment Squadron (Medium) (red)
326th Bombardment Squadron (Medium) (blue and white)
327th Bombardment Squadron (Medium) (yellow)

98th Bombardment Group (Medium) (Square H)
Yokota Air Base, Japan
August 1950 to July 1954
342nd Bombardment Squadron (Medium)
343rd Bombardment Squadron (Medium) (red)
344th Bombardment Squadron (Medium) (green)
345th Bombardment Squadron (Medium) (white and red)

307th Bombardment Group (Square Y)
Kadena Air Base, Okinawa
August 1950 to November 1954
370th Bombardment Squadron (Medium) (red)
371st Bombardment Squadron (Medium) (yellow)
372nd Bombardment Squadron (Medium) (blue)

3rd Radar Calibration Detachment
Kadena Air Base, Okinawa
January 1950 to June 1951

10th Radar Calibration Detachment (later Squadron)
Komaki and Yokota Air Bases, Japan
January 1950 to July 1953 (moved from Komaki to Yokota and merged with
3rd Radar Calibration Det in June 1951)

512th Weather Reconnaissance Squadron (Very Long Range)
(RB-29, WB-29)
Yokota and Misawa Air Bases, Japan
June 1950 to February 1951

56th Strategic Reconnaissance Squadron (Medium)
(RB-29)
Misawa Air Base, Japan
February 1951 to July 1953

514th Weather Reconnaissance Squadron (Very Long Range)
(RB-29, WB-29)
Andersen Air Force Base, Guam
June 1950 to February 1951

54th Weather Reconnaissance Squadron
(RB-29, WB-29, WB-50)
Andersen Air Force Base, Guam
1947 to 1974

2nd Air Rescue Squadron
(D flight equipped with SB-29)
Kadena Air Base, Okinawa
circa 1951 to 1953

34th Air Rescue Squadron
(SB-29)

37th Air Rescue Squadron
(SB-29)

43rd Air Refueling Squadron
(KB-29P/M)

91st Strategic Reconnaissance Squadron (Circle X)
(RB-29, RB-50G)
Yokota and Johnson Air Bases, Japan
January 1950 to circa July 1953 (reinforced on 16 November 1950 when it
absorbed the 31st SRS, and in August 1951 by Detachment 3 with RB-50Gs)

581st Air Resupply and Communication Wing
(B-29)
Clark Field, the Philippines
January 1953 to post-war

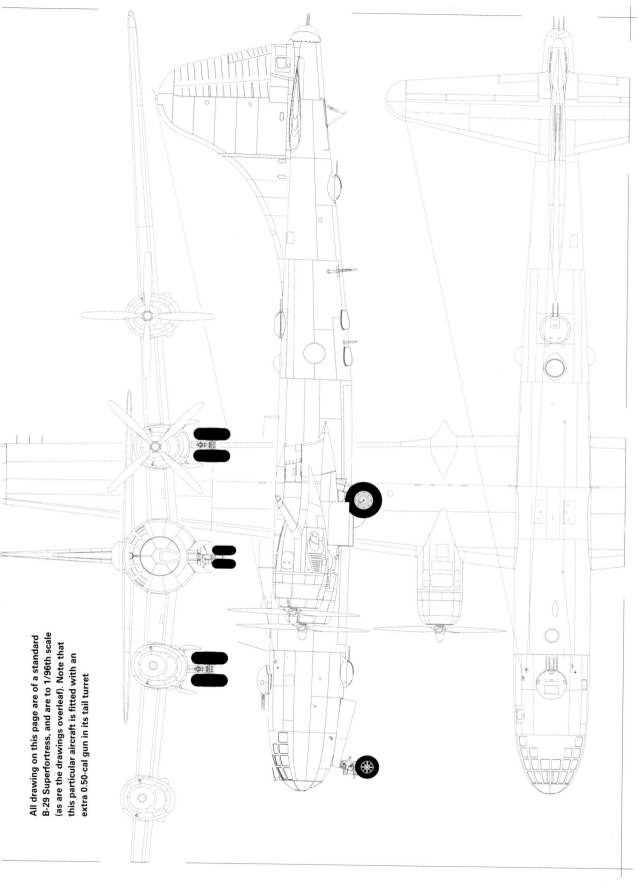

All drawing on this page are of a standard
B-29 Superfortress, and are to 1/96th scale
(as are the drawings overleaf). Note that
this particular aircraft is fitted with an
extra 0.50-cal gun in its tail turret

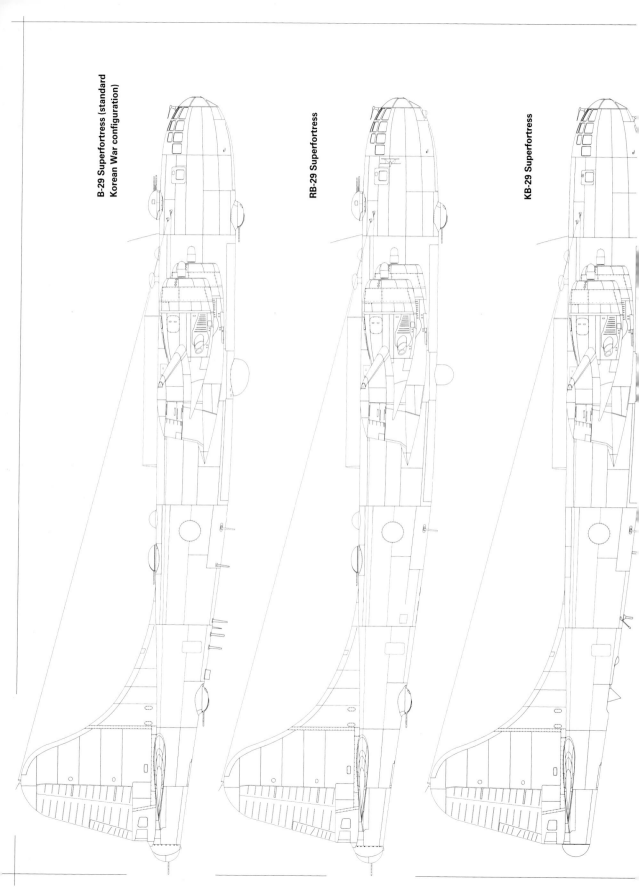

B-29 Superfortress (standard Korean War configuration)

RB-29 Superfortress

KB-29 Superfortress

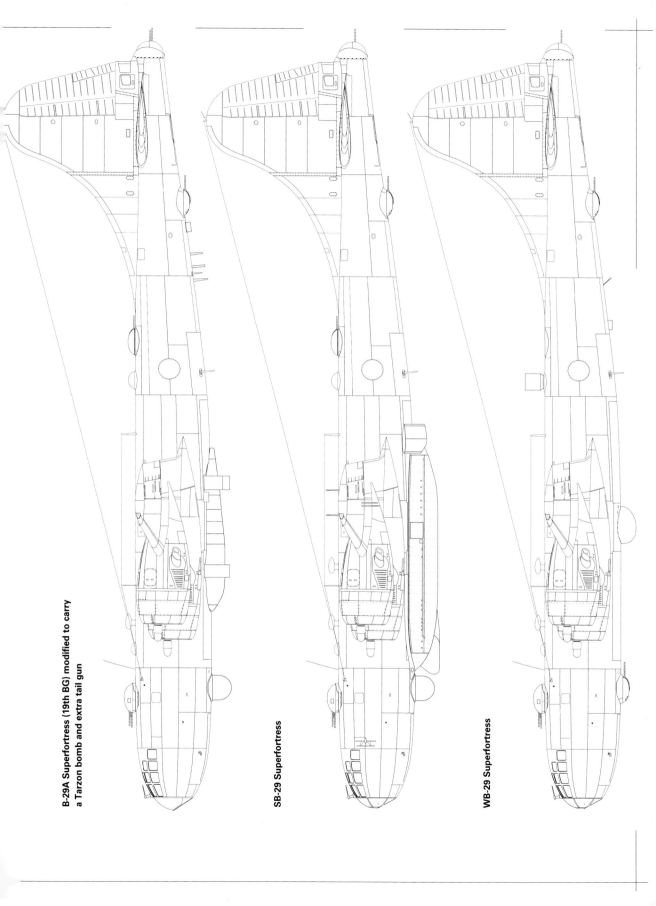

B-29A Superfortress (19th BG) modified to carry
a Tarzon bomb and extra tail gun

SB-29 Superfortress

WB-29 Superfortress

COLOUR PLATES

General notes on artwork.

Covering almost all the individual squadrons within the bomb groups that served in Korea, this colour section depicts B-29s marked with the correct squadron colours for the first time thanks to the information supplied by veterans. Where names of crew members appear on aircraft, it can be safely assumed that other names were worn near the remaining crew stations – unless photographic evidence exists, these details are not indicated on the profiles. Where markings existed on both sides of a nose, details are reproduced on the nose art pages. Many 'standard' markings varied in style from bomber to bomber – these include the USAF logo, serial numbers and the many warning/information stencils. The national insignia varied depending on which plant produced a particular bomber. Technical details also varied, in particular the ventral ECM and radar fittings. The nose art pages show nose gear doors extended to better illustrate the markings applied.

1

B-29A-40-BN 44-61656 *CREAM OF THE CROP* **of the 30th BS/19th BG, Kadena, Okinawa, 8 March 1951**

The 19th BG utilised coloured nose bands, nose gear doors, wing tips and fin tips (blue represented the 30th BS) together with a horizontal black band on the fin. Some aircraft also had a section of the centre fuselage above the wing roots painted in the squadron colour. Each squadron placed their insignia on the fin – in this case a version of 'Finnegan the Cop' on a yellow disc edged in black. *CREAM OF THE CROP* was shot down by a MiG-15 on 22 October 1951 whilst being flown by the Capt Lyle B Bordeaux crew. Its No 1 engine and hydraulic system knocked out, the aircraft was abandoned over the Yellow Sea. The entire crew was rescued by the 3rd ARS.

2

B-29A-40-BN 44-61749 *SOUTHERN COMFORT* **of the 30th BS/19th BG, Kadena, Okinawa, September 1950**

Formerly known as *City of Houston*, 44-61749 had flown with the 19th BG in World War 2. The blue squadron colour is unusually light, whilst the last four digits of the radio call number appear on the nose gear doors. One of at least two B-29s to wear the name *SOUTHERN COMFORT* in Korea, 44-61749 was lost in combat on 19 September 1950.

3

B-29-70-BW 44-69959 *BUB* **of the 30th BS/19th BG, Kadena, Okinawa, September 1951**

Wearing the 30th BS's blue trim, this aircraft's full nickname was *Beat Up Bastard*, abbreviated by the crew to *BUB*. The latter made reference to the fact that this was one of the oldest B-29s to see combat in Korea. Assigned to Gunnar Johnston and his crew between May and December 1951, *BUB's* demise is remembered by tail gunner Joe Larimore. '*BUB* made its sunset trip to the states, where it crashed, with loss of life, at Barksdale AFB in December 1951. It stalled approximately half a mile before reaching the runway. The only crewman I remember was a Cajun named Fleming, who survived largely unscathed'.

4

B-29A-50-BN 44-61835 *DRAGON LADY* **of the 30th BS/19th BG, Kadena, Okinawa, April 1951**

It was common practice during the Korean era for B-29s to carry an individual name and/or nose art on the starboard side, whilst the port side usually carried a group crest and mission record. Like most 19th BG aeroplanes, *DRAGON LADY* wore the unit's crest, which incorporates a yellow winged sword within four stars (the square of the constellation of Pegasus). The azure background was often seen rendered in black, especially on aircraft with black undersides. The group's motto *IN ALIS VINCIMUS* (On Wings We Conquer) appears above. The bomber wears 82 mission markings, some of which have red fins to indicate lead missions. Five MiG kills also appear above the mission tally. *DRAGON LADY* was attacked by MiGs on 12 April 1951 whilst being piloted by Capt Howard R Sproul. With damage to the vertical stabiliser and cockpit windows, the bomber made an emergency landing at Suwon Air Base. Sproul, and 2Lt Gene E Wright lost their lives, while 1Lt Willis E Umholtz was wounded. The aircraft duly returned to action, only to sustain heavy battle damage on 31 October 1951. The No 3 engine caught fire and then the right wing tore off, causing the bomber to crash north of Kadena. All 12 crewmen on board the bomber perished.

5

B-29A-65-BN 44-62166 *Fujigmo* **of the 93rd BS/19th BG, Kadena, Okinawa, 1950**

'FUJIGMO' was a term used by American airmen when their tour of duty was nearing its end. The acronym stood for 'Fuck yoU Jack, I Got My Orders', which meant the individual concerned had received his assignment orders to go home. Below the name *Fujigmo* is a yellow and blue shield incorporating a 'sword' (a purple shaft), a fist with a raised finger and the half moon (an outhouse decoration). *Fujigmo's* combat career ended after it had been transferred to the 307th BW, the bomber experiencing an engine fire on 22 July 1952. The B-29 exploded and crashed north-east of Ocho-o, South Korea, Capt Leroy E Aschenbrenner and his entire crew being killed. The aircraft is depicted as it appeared whilst with the 93rd BS, wearing the unit's red trim and 'screaming indian' insignia.

6

B-29-50-MO 44-86323 *FOUR-A-BREAST* of Capt Glenn Garig, 30th BS/19th BG, Kadena, Okinawa, November 1951

This aircraft was originally to have been called something else, according to an anonymous B-29 crewmember who was part of its crew. 'This nose art inspired our crew to name our aeroplane, *Cluster Phobia*. We were going to depict four "SYTs" (Sweet Young Things), with Air Medals dangling from their most prominent points. Alas, the artwork for *Cluster Phobia* was never finished. I later heard that "our" B-29 was shot down shortly after we left Okinawa'.

7

B-29-80-BW 44-70134 *NO SWEAT!* of the 93rd BS/19th BG, Kadena, Okinawa, September 1952

'Bud' Farrell served in the 93rd BS as a gunner, and during his tour he sortied in numerous B-29s, including *NO SWEAT!* 'I crewed seven or eight of our eleven ships while I was at Kadena – 802 (44-69802 *Bait Me*), 002, 012, 359 (44-86359 *Capt Sam and Ten Scents*), 007 (44-70007 *Target for Tonight*), 751 (44-61751 *Lubricating Lady*), 705 and 134 including *NO SWEAT!*. The latter was our primary ship for most of our missions in the late summer and autumn months of 1952. Our crew, led by Capt Brooke Cheney, flew 25 missions over North Korea, with several being "max efforts" to Pyongyang. Our daylight raids took us to the Chinese 5th Army HQ and airfield at Yonpo, to Sinuiju's Oriental Light Metals Works, the Suiho Dam and the Namsan-Ni Chemical Plant, all of which were situated on the Yalu River, and within sight of the MiG base at Antung. On the Suiho mission, *Bait Me*, which was immediately behind us, augered in from severe icing south of the 38th Parallel. Then we lost a 307th ship immediately in front of us over the dam, and at least five other B-29s in the stream took flak damage'.

8

B-29-85-BW 44-87657 *COMMAND DECISION* of Capt Donald M Kovic, 28th BS/19th BG Kadena, Okinawa, July 1953

COMMAND DECISION appears in the green trim representing the 28th BS, its jet black undersides extending up to cover the entire fin – this style of camouflage was used late in the war by the 19th BG. Clyde Durham flew this aircraft near war's end. 'On our third combat mission we were assigned to fly *COMMAND DECISION*, which was arguably the most famous B-29 of the Korean War. It had completed many combat missions over Japan in World War 2 and now also over Korea, and had become famous in the latter conflict for the five MiG kills credited to its gunners. Its aircraft commander at that time was Capt Donald Kovic, who signed up for another tour when his crew's tour of duty was up. Promoted to major, he became the unit's Operations Officer. There was a popular story told at the time about the MiG victories – it was said that Capt Kovic and the crew

were on a daylight mission when they shot at two MiGs, claimed three, got credit for four and then painted five kills on their B-29. Of course, this was said with one's tongue planted firmly in one's cheek, for other crews had verified these kills'.

9

B-29-85-BW 44-87661 *KOZA KID* of the 30th BS/19th BG, Kadena, Okinawa, September 1950

Another veteran of World War 2, 44-87661 was known as *American Beauty III* when assigned to the 794th BS/468th BG. In Korea the aeroplane carried this name and ugly face, its previous name being replaced by the word 'Ugly'. The bomber was later renamed *KOZA KID*, but following complaints, it was again changed to *Night-Mare!*. According to the aircraft crew chief, Airman 1st Class Jim Stark, Koza was the name of a village just outside the main gate at Kadena. 44-87661 survived the Korean War and returned safely to the US.

10

B-29-97-BW 45-21746 *RAZ'N HELL* of the 28th BS/19th BG, Kadena, Okinawa, September 1951

Three 19th BG B-29s were modified to carry the Razon and Tarzon bombs – 45-21745 *Lucifer* of the 30th BS, 45-21746 *RAZ'N HELL* of the 28th BS and 45-21749 (name unknown) of the 93rd BS. The modifications saw the centre section and bomb-bay doors cut away, the radome relocated to the lower forward turret position and the fitment of a B-50-style nose cone. The Razon/Tarzon programme was terminated due to safety reasons, and *RAZ'N HELL* was returned to standard B-29 configuration as depicted here. Following fire damage, it was reworked and eventually sent back to Korea to serve with the 307th BG. *RAZ'N HELL* completed its combat tour and returned to the US in 1953. In addition to *RAZ'N HELL*'s nose art (painted by Cpl Dick Thompson), a Kilroy character appears near the flight engineer's station.

11

B-29-35-MO 44-27263 *MISSION INN* of the 2nd BS/22nd BG, Kadena, Okinawa, October 1950

B-29 44-27263 was named after the historical Mission Inn in Riverside, California, close to March AFB (home of the 22nd BG). During its Korean service, the aeroplane initially retained the group's 'Triangle I' marking, but this was replaced by the 'Circle E' tail code. The squadron colours, which were applied to the bombers' fin tips, were red for the 2nd BS, blue for the 19th BS and yellow for the 33rd BS. The group also continued the SAC practice of adorning tails with the appropriate USAF insignia – in this instance the Fifteenth Air Force. Some 22nd BG B-29s also wore the group's crest, comprising a cougar's left paw on an azure background, below which appeared the motto *"DUCEMUS"* ('We Lead'). *MISSION INN* remained in-theatre when the 22nd BG went home in October 1950, the bomber having been transferred to the 28th BS/19th BG.

12

B-29A-60-BN 44-62060 *Spirit of Freeport* of the 19th BS/22nd BG, Kadena, Okinawa, October 1950
Legend has it that the construction of *Spirit of Freeport* (a veteran of World War 2) was paid for in part by the citizens of Freeport, Long Island. However, a B-29 crewman from the Korean War claims, that the name had been retained by the aircraft since World War 2, and that it refers to the hamlet of Freeport in Brazoria Country, Texas. When the 22nd BG returned to the US in the autumn of 1950, *Spirit of Freeport* joined the 307th BG, with whom it remained until war's end.

13

B-29-40-MO 44-86261 *MULE TRAIN* of Maj George Ham, 33rd BS/22nd BG, Kadena, Okinawa, October 1950
A product of Omaha's Glenn L Martin factory, *MULE TRAIN* wears the yellow fin tip marking of the 33rd BS, but lacks the coloured nose gear doors. The absence of part of the tail number and Circle E indicates that a new rudder has been installed. One B-29 veteran remembers that the Frankie Laine song 'Mule Train' (sung by Vaughn Monroe in the film *Singing Guns* and by Gene Autry in *Mule Train*) was so popular in the war zone that Armed Forces Radio once played it for 24 hours without a break! The bomber, named after the song, apparently survived the 22nd BG's relatively brief presence in the conflict and returned safely to the United States.

14

B-29-50-MO 44-86349 *"JOHNS OTHER WIFE"* of the 33rd BS/22nd BG, Kadena, Okinawa, October 1950
"JOHNS OTHER WIFE" began the war with the 22nd BG, as shown here. The B-29 features the group's Circle E and ubiquitous Fifteenth Air Force emblem on the fin. *"JOHNS OTHER WIFE"* remained in combat after the 22nd BG went home, fighting on with the 28th BS/19th BG. Depicted whilst assigned to the 22nd BG, it has the 33rd BS's yellow trim and yellow nose wheel doors.

15

B-29-40-MO 44-27332 *MISS SPOKANE* of Lt Col Pomas B Fasules, 326th BS/92nd BG, Yokota, Japan, October 1951
Adorned with 90 bomb silhouettes on its nose, *MISS SPOKANE* took its name from the 92nd BG's home base in Spokane, Washington. Aside from wearing the 'circle W' tail code, the bomber also employs blue trim with white stripes as a squadron marking. The other units in the group used red (325th BS) and yellow (327th) trim. Some B-29s also featured the unofficial group insignia on the port side of the nose, this marking consisting of a bomb superimposed on a map of Korea. Finally, a number of 92nd BG bombers had their nose cone framing painted in squadron colours, but this marking system does not appear to have been consistent, and was also seen on some 19th,

98th and 307th aircraft. The son of *MISS SPOKANE's* pilot remembered the bomber well. 'My late father, Lt Col Pomas B Fasules, was very proud of his military service. He was a Pearl Harbor survivor who had been born on 4 July, and he flew 38 combat missions in World War 2 and 38 in Korea. He was flying *MISS SPOKANE* on 13 October 1951 when it was damaged by flak over Sunan, North Korea'.

16

B-29A-65-BN 44-61790 *PEACE ON EARTH* of the 326th BS/92nd BG, Yokota, Japan, October 1951
One of several B-29s to have been named *PEACE ON EARTH*, 44-61790 is seen adorned with 15 bomb silhouettes on its nose. It too wears the blue trim with white stripes that the 326th BS used during the early months of the Korean conflict. The 92nd returned to the US in the autumn of that year, but most of its bombers transferred to other units and remained in the combat zone.

17

B-29A-70-BN 44-62224 *THE WANDERER* of the 326th BS/92nd BG, Yokota, Japan, October 1951
S/Sgt James S Peters of the 325th BS remembers when the distinctive nose art applied to this B-29 was seen for the first time. 'I was on the flightline when the nose art was unveiled. The CO of the 326th was Lt Col Ralph M Wanderer, who was not particularly liked by the pilot of 44-62224. The latter had a Japanese artist apply the nose art, and if you looked closely at the painting the "butterflies" were actually the insignia of a full colonel (Eagles) and the "Wanderer" was a caricature of a "bum" with a butterfly net, chasing the "butterflies". Everyone was called onto the flightline to witness the unveiling of the nose art – the entire Maintenance Control and HQ personnel were there as well. Lt Col Wanderer was standing there with a very red face. He contrived to leave *THE WANDERER* at Yokota with the 98th BG when we left for home, as he would absolutely NOT allow the B-29 to fly back to the states when the 92nd BG returned from its four-month TDY'.

18

B-29-65-BW 44-69805 *"DEAL ME IN"* of the 325th BS/92nd BG, Yokota, Japan, 1950
B-29 *"DEAL ME IN"* (aka *Miss Bea Havin*) is seen here with the red trim assigned to the 325th BS, as well as the rare coloured nose cone framing. The artwork on this aircraft was described by one veteran as having been inspired by cartoonist Milton Caniff. Like many of the 92nd BG B-29s, 44-69805 was later reassigned to the 98th BG. On 14 October 1951 it was hit by flak and the bale-out order given, then cancelled. By then, however, three crewmembers had jumped out over Sagami Bay, Japan, and these men lost their lives.

19

B-29-60-MO 44-86438 *FLYING PARTS* of the 327th BS/92nd BG, Yokota, Japan, 1950

Omaha-built Superfortress 44-86438 (a product of a factory for which records on constructor's numbers are unavailable) was named *FLYING PARTS*, and it wore black undersides long before the MiG threat forced B-29s to fly most of their missions at night. The bomber also features the yellow trim assigned to the 327th BS. The eventual disposition of this aircraft is not indicated in the aircraft record card maintained by the USAF History Office, but *FLYING PARTS* is assumed to have survived the Korean War.

20

B-29-40-MO 44-27341 *Dreamer* of the 343rd BS/ 98th BG, Yokota, Japan, January 1951
At the start of its Korean service, the 98th was the only B-29 group to use a side number marking system. A letter denoting the squadron was used, as well as the usual unit colour – red trim for the 343rd BS, as well as the letter A, green trim and the letter B for the 344th BS and white/red stripes and the letter C for the 345th BS. The letter was followed by the last three digits of the serial to serve as an aircraft identifier ('buzz number'). *Dreamer* sustained serious flak damage on 3 January 1951 while attacking a bridge at Kogungong-dong.

21

B-29A-40-BN 44-61676 *SAD SAC* of Capt Anthony M Carson, 343rd BS/98th BG, Yokota, Japan, 1951
'Sad Sack' was a cartoon character representing a US soldier of the draft era who seemed unable to shape up. George Baker, an experienced Walt Disney studio cartoonist, and later a World War 2 veteran, created the character who first appeared in *Life* magazine in 1941. SAC was the acronym for Strategic Air Command, of which the 98th BG was a part. As well as the standard trim colour areas, *SAD SAC* also has the coloured nose cone seen on a few 98th BG B-29s. On the port side of the nose are 53 bomb silhouettes, together with the 98th BG crest. The latter takes the form of an indented diagonal line flanked by a mailed hand grasping a bomb on one side and an olive wreath on the other. Beneath this is the group motto, 'Force For Freedom'. Further aft is the 343rd BS insignia, along with the motto 'Couldn't Care Less'.

22

B-29A-50-BN 44-61830 *EVERY MAN A "Tiger"* of the 343rd BS/98th BG, Yokota, Japan, February 1951
'Every Man A Tiger' was the motto for fledgling fighter pilots entering gunnery school at Nellis AFB, Nevada. The appearance of the slogan on a bomber may have been a dig at fighter pilots who, when MiGs first showed up in Korean skies, were able to do little to protect beleaguered bomber crews. Both American and Soviet sources state that this B-29 was shot down by a MiG-15 on 1 March 1951 over Kogungong-dong. A former 92nd BG B-29, 44-61830 appears with the red trim of the 343rd BS/92nd BG.

23

B-29A-50-BN 44-61872 *ACE IN THE HOLE* of the 343rd BS/98th BG, Yokota, Japan, 1952
B-29 44-61872 was originally named *ACE IN THE HOLE*, but following the application of black undersides it wore two versions of the name *Sac's Appeal*. The bomber was damaged by flak on 22 April 1952 and crash-landed at Kimpo, in South Korea, without sustaining casualties. Like many 98th BG aircraft, *ACE IN THE HOLE* was previously assigned to the 92nd BG. Indeed, its nose art was applied by the same artist that had painted the group's B-29 44-69805 *"DEAL ME IN"*. In fact, he used the same five playing cards for both bomber's, with the ace reversed in an attempt at subtlety. The words *Deal Me In* also appeared in small letters below the artwork, which has caused confusion relating to the identity of this B-29.

24

B-29A-60-BN 44-62106 *READY WILLIN WANTON* of Lt Art Fink, 345th BS/98th BG, Yokota, Japan, August 1952
T/Sgt Bill Banks was the crew chief for *READY WILLING WANTON* from December 1951 through to August 1952, and he remembers, 'The aeroplane I crewed had been overhauled and revised with some new equipment such as Loran, which was state of the art at that time. We had switched to B-36s shortly after the war started, but my experience as a B-29 ground crew chief became critical in Japan so away I went. I was happy, as I had spent nearly three years on B-29s, and liked them a lot more than the mechanically nightmarish B-36. This aircraft was a good one, never aborting a mission due to mechanical problems while I was crew chief'. *READY WILLING WANTON* is depicted here after it had flown 105 missions and claimed one MiG-15 kill. Originally named *Chief Mac's 10 Little Indians*, 44-62106 is adorned with the markings of the 345th BS – two red stripes on a white fin tip and three black stripes on the white nose gear doors (the centre one broken by the buzz number). The group letter H has been added to a previous circle group marking, giving the non-standard 'circle H' as sometimes seen on 98th BG B-29s.

25

B-29A-70-BN 44-62261 *NIP ON NEES* of the 344th BS/98th BG, Yokota, Japan, late 1951
Superfortress 44-62261 (c/n 11738) wears the green trim of the 344th BS, together with the black undersides that became routine after October 1951. It also has the non-standard 'circle H' marking representing the 98th BG. At least three Superfortresses during the Korean War had names based on the word 'Nipponese', slang for Japanese. The name was a word play on Nihon, the Japanese language word for Japan.

26

B-29A-70-BN 44-62281 *FIRE BALL* of the 345th BS/ 98th BG, Yokota, Japan, May 1951

Piloted by Capt James Comfort, B-29A-70-BN 44-62281 (c/n 11758) was hit by flak on 7 May 1951 and struggled back to make a shaky landing at Yokota. Repaired, it remained in frontline service well into 1952. This Renton-built Superfortress initially featured a caricature of *Woody Woodpecker* on its nose, although this was later modified through the addition of a horn in his grasp and the application of an undressing female further forward.

27

B-29-55-BW 44-69667 *SNUGGLEBUNNY* of the 343rd BS/98th BG, Yokota, Japan, 1951
SNUGGLEBUNNY, like many Korean War Superfortresses, was initially blooded during World War 2 whilst serving with the 40th BS/6th BG and the 39th BS/6th BG – the bomber flew 65 missions in the campaign against Japan. The 'Snugglebunny' appellation dates back to the Pacific War. Built in Wichita by Boeing, *SNUGGLEBUNNY* features the red fin tip and nose wheel doors associated with the 343rd BS, while the non-standard A-667 'buzz number' is the early style marking of the 98th BG. *SNUGGLEBUNNY* flew a further 85 missions in Korea, and was also credited with a MiG-15 kill.

28

B-29-60-BW 44-69800 *BEETLE BOMBER* of the 344th BS/98th BG, Yokota, Japan, 1951
Another World War 2 veteran, 44-89800 was previously assigned to the 458th BS/330th BG as *City of San Francisco*, with whom it flew 26 missions against Japan (see *Osprey Combat Aircraft 33 - B-29 Superfortress Units of World War 2* for details). Initially named *BEETLE BOMB*, with a cartoon beetle artwork, by the 344th, this was later modified to *BEETLE BOMBER* – a female figure was also added. The B-29 has the green trim (and painted nose cone framing) of the 344th BS.

29

B-29-45-MO 44-86284 *DOWNS' CLOWNS* of the 343rd BS/98th BG, Yokota, Japan, 1951
Colourfully festooned with the smiling face of a circus entertainer, this Omaha-built B-29-45-MO Superfortress served with the 98th BG at Yokota. The red fin tip and nose wheel doors were associated with the 343rd BS, and this aircraft also boasts a non-standard 'circle H' marking, denoting its assignment to the 98th BG.

30

B-29-50-MO 44-86340 *WOLF PACK* of the 345th BS/98th BG, Yokota, Japan, 1951
WOLF PACK was one of many Korean era B-29s which had changes made to its nose art whilst in service. The original wolf, in its suit and top hat, saw his apparel change into a dress uniform. The 'frame' was removed and the name enlarged (see nose art gallery), and a running woman added to the right of the wolf. The bomber was assigned to the 345th BS, and it survived the war. An

instrument panel from this machine is currently on display within the USAF Museum in Dayton, Ohio.

31

B-29-55-MO 44-86415 *MISS MINOOKI/SQUEEZE PLAY* of the 343rd BS/98th BG, Yokota, Japan, 1951
B-29 44-86415 of the 343rd BS was unusual in having a different name and artwork on either side of its nose. *MISS MINOOKI* appears on the port side, along with the 98th BG insignia, whilst *SQUEEZE PLAY* appeared on the starboard side (see nose art gallery). A 'squeeze play' occurs in baseball when the batter attempts to bunt so the runner on third base may score. Coupled with the 'washer woman' having an accident, this was one of the more amusing name and nose art combinations to be seen on a Korean War B-29.

32

B-29-90-BW 45-21721 *TAIL WIND* of the 345th BS/98th BG, Yokota, Japan, 1951
TAIL WIND was Wichita-built B-29-90-BW 45-21721 (c/n 13615), the bomber being amongst the last Superfortresses produced by Boeing. Serving with the 345th BS/98th BG at Yokota, the B-29 wore the white fin tip with red stripes that was the assigned marking of its squadron. This aircraft was lost on 7 February 1952 when it flew into a hill north-east of Yokota, killing its entire crew.

33

B-29-95-BW 45-21822 *HEAVENLY LADEN* of Capt Raymond M Lajeunesse, 344th BS/98th BW, Yokota, Japan, 1951
On 1 April 1951, the 98th BW deployed to Yokota, where it assumed the tactical role of the 98th BG. One of the aircraft it assumed control of was *HEAVENLY LADEN*, seen here in the green trim of the 344th BS. Manufactured in Wichita near the end of World War 2, this aircraft also boasted a Kilroy character near the flight engineer's station in a similar style to *RAZ'N HELL* (profile 10). *HEAVENLY LADEN* flew a considerable number of missions before coming to an untimely end on 29 January 1952, when it suffered an engine fire and crashed five miles west of Yokohama. The crew all baled out successfully.

34

RB-29A-20-BN 42-94000 *TIGER LIL* of Capt Torrey, 91st SRS/55th SRW, Yokota, Japan, June 1950
Wayland Mayo was an Aerial Photo Gunner with the Capt Torrey's crew, and he flew *TIGER LIL* on no fewer than 50 successful missions. He later researched the demise of the aeroplane during a Cold War incident. 'On 7 November 1954, *TIGER LIL* was shot down by Soviet fighters, flown by pilots Kostin and Seberyakov, near Hokkaido Island, Japan. The aeroplane, carrying a crew of 11, was conducting a routine photographic reconnaissance flight near Hokkaido and the southern most islands within the Kurile chain. The aeroplane was attacked and seriously

damaged, forcing the crew to bale out. Ten were successfully rescued after landing in the sea, but the eleventh man drowned when he became entangled in his parachute lines. Another report sent to me by Jess Richey of the 98th BG stated that the Russians had claimed that the RB-29 had entered Soviet airspace and fired on them. They returned fire, shooting the American aircraft down. The crew claimed that they were not over Soviet territory, and that the MiGs had fired first'.

35

RB-29A-45-BN 44-61727 *So Tired/Seven to Seven* of Capt Norman A Anderson, 91st SRS/55th SRW, Yokota, Japan 1952

CM/Sgt Don Rubendall was a member of *So Tired's* crew in 1952-53, and he remembers, 'I flew with pilot Capt Norman A Anderson, 1st Engineer Chuck Hammer, 1st photo Walt Bly, central fire controller Mervin Sinclair, right scan Jose Gaberial, radioman John Orlovsky, tail gunner Joe Shaw, navigator Mike Deleone, radar operator John Whitaker and co-pilot Rob Harder. Our crew flew *So Tired/Seven To Seven* 50 times to Korea and back, and experienced only two incidents that I can recall. The first was when the No 3 engine picked up some spent flak, nicking the prop and punching a few holes in the underside of the wing. It was nothing to worry about. And the second incident was when we lost an engine out over the Sea of Japan and had to recover at Hokkaido. Weather was almost zero-zero, and we had to have an F-80 talk us through the "V"-shaped valley approach. He tucked his nose in behind our No 4 engine and took us down. I swear to god he put a scratch on my blister! I thought he was going to put that wing tank right in my lap. Other than that, all I can say is I am truly sorry for our replacement crew and their families'. 44-61727 was shot down by Soviet MiGs near Sinanju, in North Korea, on the night of 3 July 1952 by Soviet ace Maj Anatoly Karelin, executive officer of the 351st Air Regiment. The RB-29 is seen here after it had flown 64 missions, and bearing the 91st SRS insignia (a knight on horseback chasing the devil).

36

RB-29A-55-BN 44-61929 *HONEYBUCKET HONSHOS* of the 91st SRS/55th SRW, Yokota, Japan, 1952

Markings used by the 91st SRS varied considerably during the Korean War, the unit eventually standardising on the 'Circle X' and green fin tips and nose gear doors – the latter usually had a white flash broken by the 'buzz number'. Seen late in the war, 44-61929 also has black undersides. The nose art saw at least three crew name changes and detail variation, although the logo *Dump Machine 929* remained the same.

37

B-29-65-BW 44-69816 *SIT'N'GIT* of Maj J Wilson, 371st BS/307th BW, Kadena, Okinawa, 1951

The 307th BG in effect became the 307th BW on

10 February 1951, the unit using the 'square Y' tail marking and the following squadron colours – red trim for the 370th BS, yellow for the 371st BS and blue for the 372nd BS. The size and location of the trim varied during the war, with some bombers having coloured wingtips and nose bands. Strangely, *SIT'N'GIT* nose art details show red trim, despite the aeroplane's assignment to the 371st BS. Duplication of the radio call number was a standard practice of this group, as was the application of the its crest, comprising a four-petalled dogwood bloom. Darrel Cooper was *SIT'N'GIT's* flight engineer. 'My crew were pilot Maj Jack Wilson, co-pilot 2Lt Manley P Bishop, bombardier Capt Ira Whitlock, navigator 2Lt Charles Swindell, VO Capt George Maund, flight engineer S/Sgt Darrel Cooper, Radio A/2C Charles Barksdale, ECM A/1C Dale Terry, central fire controller A/2C Robert Henry, left gunner A/2C Albert Byrnes, right gunner A/1C George Simpson and tail gunner A/2C Dale Yaney. I still have a small flag we flew outside the pilot's window when we were on the ground – it said "Wilson's Worriers"'. *SIT'N'GIT* left Kadena in November 1954 and stored at Davis-Monthan AFB, Arizona, until modified into a TB-29A. It was then assigned to the 3510th Combat Crew Training Wing at Randolph AFB, Texas, in July 1955. The bomber was lost in a collision with an F-86D fighter over Florida on 19 December 1955.

38

KB-29M-35-MO 44-27282 *TOWN PUMP* of Det 4, 43rd ARS, Yokota, Japan, 1952

Boeing's Wichita plant converted 92 B-29A/Bs into KB-29M tankers. Modifications included the removal of gun turrets and the installation of a 2300-gal jettisonable fuel tank in the bomb-bay. To complete the refuelling, a 200-ft hose, connected to a steel cable, was reeled out from a belly-mounted drum to the receiving aircraft. Although primarily designed to refuel other B-29s, the KB-29 conducted trials in Korea with RB-45s and F-84s. 44-27282 is painted in typical 43rd ARS markings, comprising a 'circle K' on the tail and a blue and white fuselage band and nose gear trim.

39

SB-29 44-70089 of Flight D, 2nd ARS, Kadena, Okinawa, April 1952

The four SB-29s assigned to Flight D, 2nd ARS flew escort missions for the bomb groups. They orbited off Kadena until the last B-29 had taken off, then escorted them to Korea. Upon their return, the SB-29s would again orbit until the bombers had landed. Missions to Korea were flown unarmed to offset the high drag of the K-3 lifeboat. The SB-29s also responded to other types of aircraft that had come down in the sea. There were a total of 25 SB-29 conversions – 44-69957, -69971, -70119, -84030, -84078, -84084, -84086, -84088, -84112, -86303, -86308, -87644, -87665, -27308, -62190, -62194, -62210, -70089, -70101, -70117, -70131, -84034, -84096, -86259 and -86355.